# FLOWERS

## GAIL GIBBONS

Holiday House  New York

## To Veronica Walsh

Special thanks to Becky Sideman, horticulture specialist
at the University of New Hampshire in Durham.

Copyright © 2018 by Gail Gibbons
All Rights Reserved
HOLIDAY HOUSE is registered in the U.S. Patent
and Trademark Office
Printed and bound in December 2017
at Toppan Leefung, DongGuan City, China.
The artwork was created on watercolor paper with
black ink, watercolors, and colored pencil.
www.holidayhouse.com
First Edition
1 3 5 7 9 10 8 6 4 2

Library of Congress Cataloging-in-Publication Data
Names: Gibbons, Gail, author.
Title: Flowers / Gail Gibbons.
Description: First edition. | New York : Holiday House, [2019]
Identifiers: LCCN 2017022477 | ISBN 9780823437870 (hardcover)
Subjects: LCSH: Flowers—Juvenile literature.
Classification: LCC SB406.5 .G53 2019 | DDC 635.9—dc23 LC record available
at https://lccn.loc.gov/2017022477

Look at all the flowers! Each kind of flower has its own unique color, size, and shape.

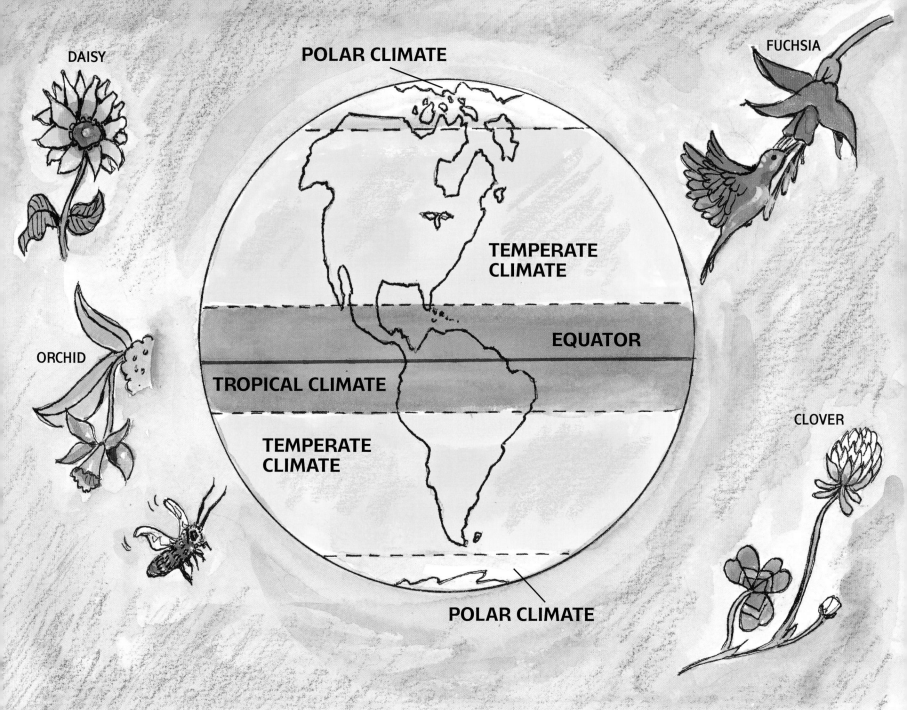

DAISY

POLAR CLIMATE

FUCHSIA

TEMPERATE
CLIMATE

ORCHID

EQUATOR

TROPICAL CLIMATE

CLOVER

TEMPERATE
CLIMATE

POLAR CLIMATE

Flowers grow in many places. Some flowers grow in temperate climates where there are four seasons. They grow only when it is not too cold. In tropical climates flowers can live longer because it is always warm.

PANSIES

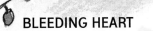

WISTERIA

# TEMPERATE CLIMATES

TEMPERATE CLIMATES have four seasons—spring, summer, fall, and winter. In winter it's too cold for flowers to survive.

HYDRANGEA

DAFFODIL

DAISY

SNAP-DRAGON

ZINNIA

POPPY

TULIP

CROCUS

DANDELIONS

DAHLIA

# TROPICAL CLIMATES

Tropical climates are always warm.

AMARYLLIS

ORCHID

BIRD-OF-PARADISE

BROMELIAD

PASSION-FLOWER

**POLAR CLIMATES** are so cold only a few plants can survive.

HIBISCUS

5

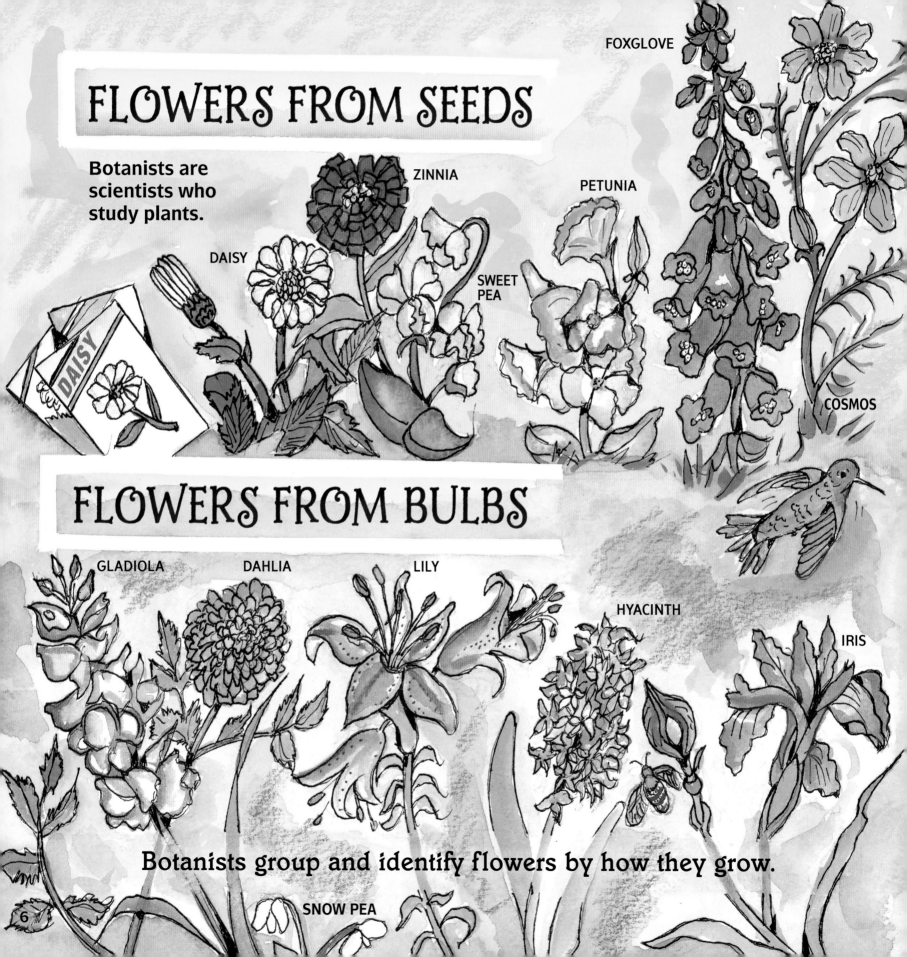

# FLOWERS FROM SEEDS

**Botanists are scientists who study plants.**

DAISY

ZINNIA

SWEET PEA

PETUNIA

FOXGLOVE

COSMOS

DAISY

# FLOWERS FROM BULBS

GLADIOLA

DAHLIA

LILY

HYACINTH

IRIS

Botanists group and identify flowers by how they grow.

SNOW PEA

6

# FLOWERS FROM VINES

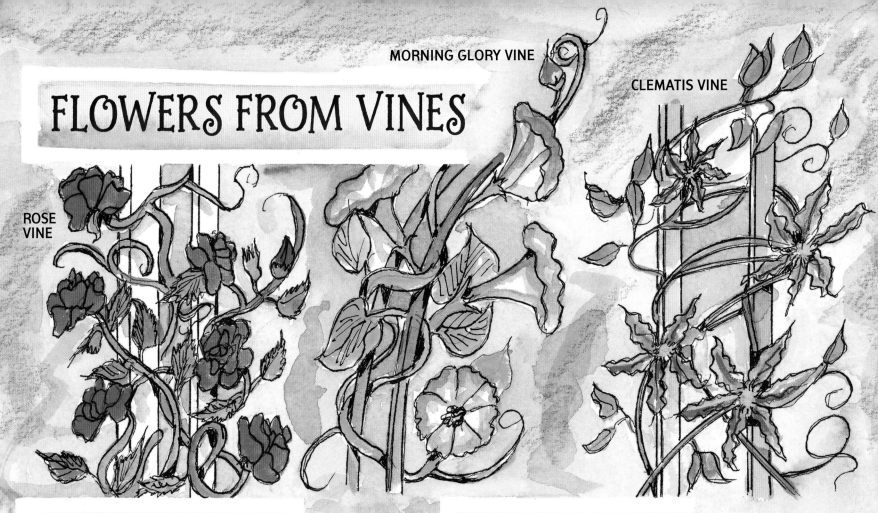

MORNING GLORY VINE

CLEMATIS VINE

ROSE VINE

# FLOWERS ON BUSHES

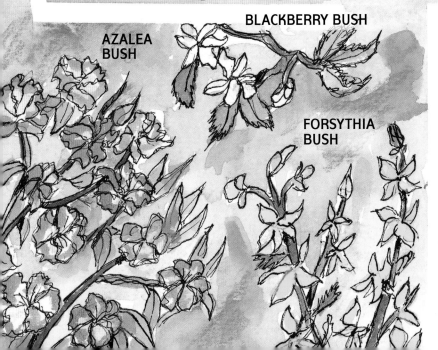

BLACKBERRY BUSH

AZALEA BUSH

FORSYTHIA BUSH

# FLOWERS ON TREES

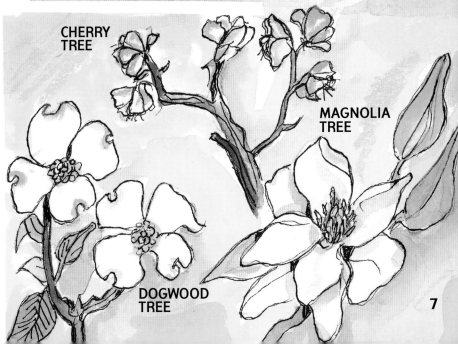

CHERRY TREE

MAGNOLIA TREE

DOGWOOD TREE

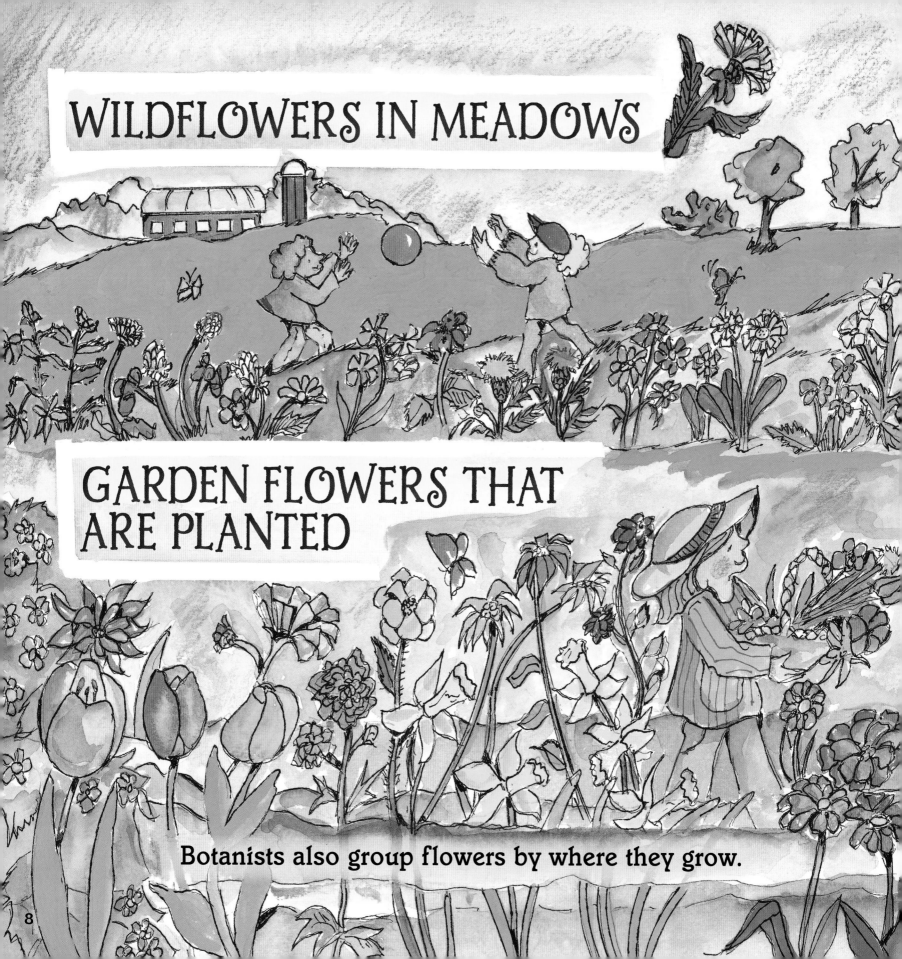

# WILDFLOWERS IN MEADOWS

# GARDEN FLOWERS THAT ARE PLANTED

Botanists also group flowers by where they grow.

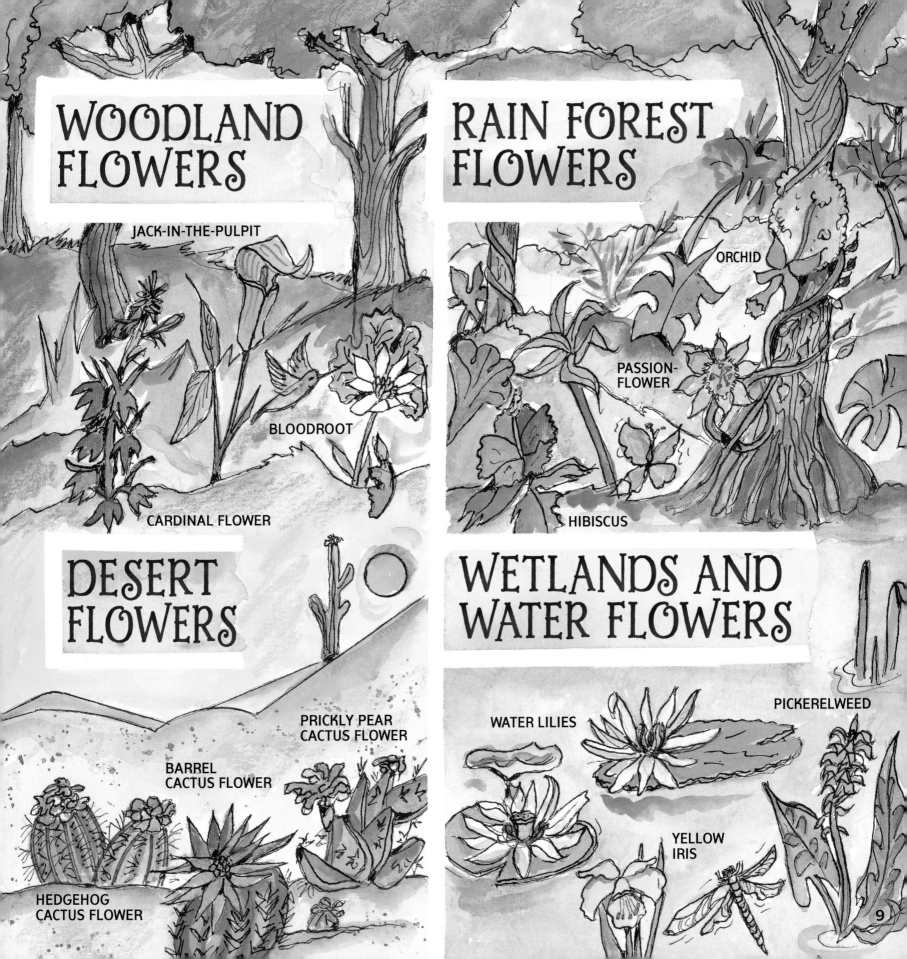

# WOODLAND FLOWERS

JACK-IN-THE-PULPIT

BLOODROOT

CARDINAL FLOWER

# RAIN FOREST FLOWERS

ORCHID

PASSION-FLOWER

HIBISCUS

# DESERT FLOWERS

PRICKLY PEAR CACTUS FLOWER

BARREL CACTUS FLOWER

HEDGEHOG CACTUS FLOWER

# WETLANDS AND WATER FLOWERS

WATER LILIES

PICKERELWEED

YELLOW IRIS

9

# A FLOWER'S ENVIRONMENT

WATER LILY

Flowers need energy to grow. This comes from sunlight and carbon dioxide, a gas in the air.

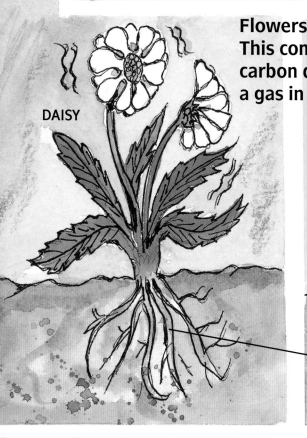

DAISY

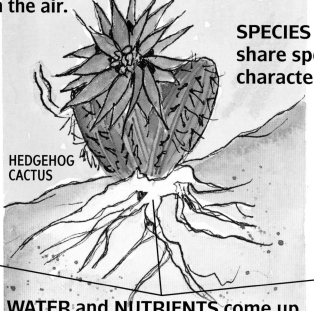

**SPECIES** share specific characteristics.

HEDGEHOG CACTUS

**WATER** and **NUTRIENTS** come up through **ROOTS**.

Some flowers grow best in SHADE.

LILY OF THE VALLEY

Others need more SUNLIGHT.

SUNFLOWER

Some flowers CLOSE AT NIGHT for PROTECTION.

CROCUS

Each species of flower grows in the environment that is best for it.

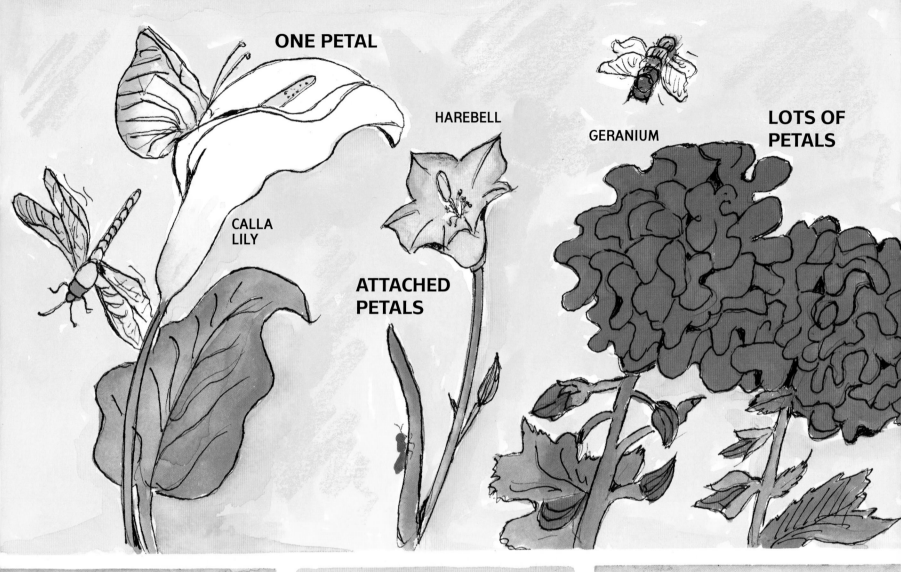

**ONE PETAL**

HAREBELL

GERANIUM

**LOTS OF PETALS**

CALLA LILY

**ATTACHED PETALS**

**ONE FLOWER growing from a stem**

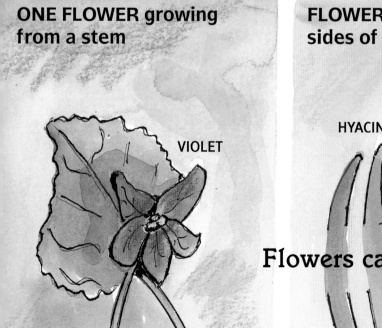

VIOLET

**FLOWERS growing from sides of a stem**

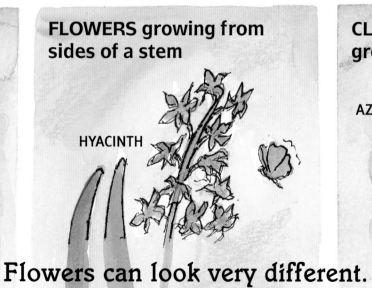

HYACINTH

**CLUSTERS OF FLOWERS growing from a stem**

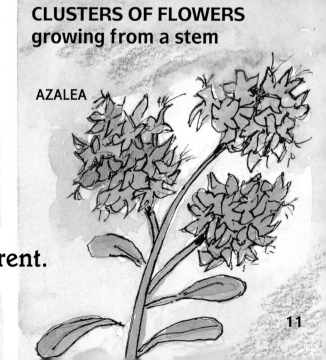

AZALEA

Flowers can look very different.

11

# ANNUAL FLOWERS

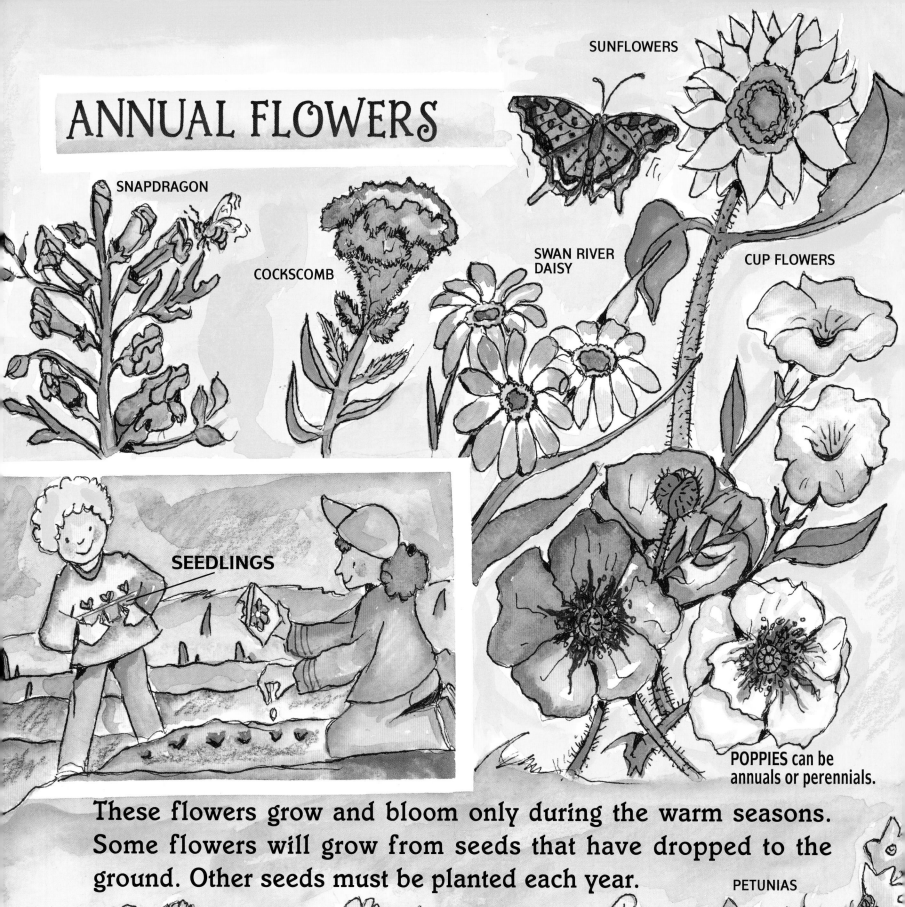

SUNFLOWERS

SNAPDRAGON

COCKSCOMB

SWAN RIVER DAISY

CUP FLOWERS

SEEDLINGS

POPPIES can be annuals or perennials.

These flowers grow and bloom only during the warm seasons. Some flowers will grow from seeds that have dropped to the ground. Other seeds must be planted each year.

PETUNIAS

# PERENNIAL FLOWERS

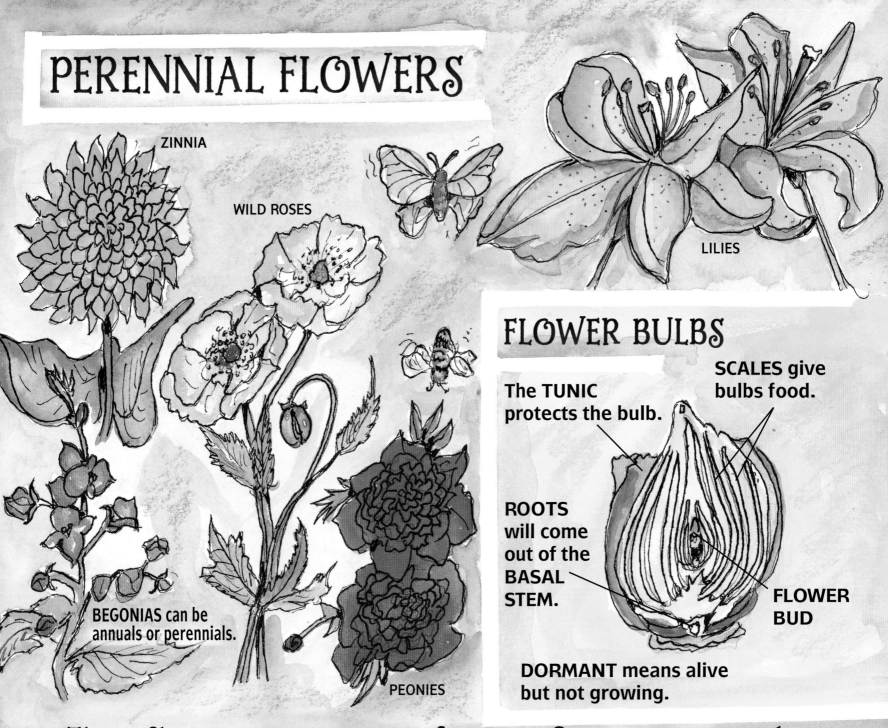

ZINNIA

WILD ROSES

LILIES

BEGONIAS can be annuals or perennials.

PEONIES

## FLOWER BULBS

The TUNIC protects the bulb.

SCALES give bulbs food.

ROOTS will come out of the BASAL STEM.

FLOWER BUD

DORMANT means alive but not growing.

These flowers come up year after year. Some start as seeds. Others began as flower bulbs. Bulbs and the roots of perennials can stay alive underground through the winter. Flowering vines, bushes, and trees are dormant through the winter.

MARSH MARIGOLDS

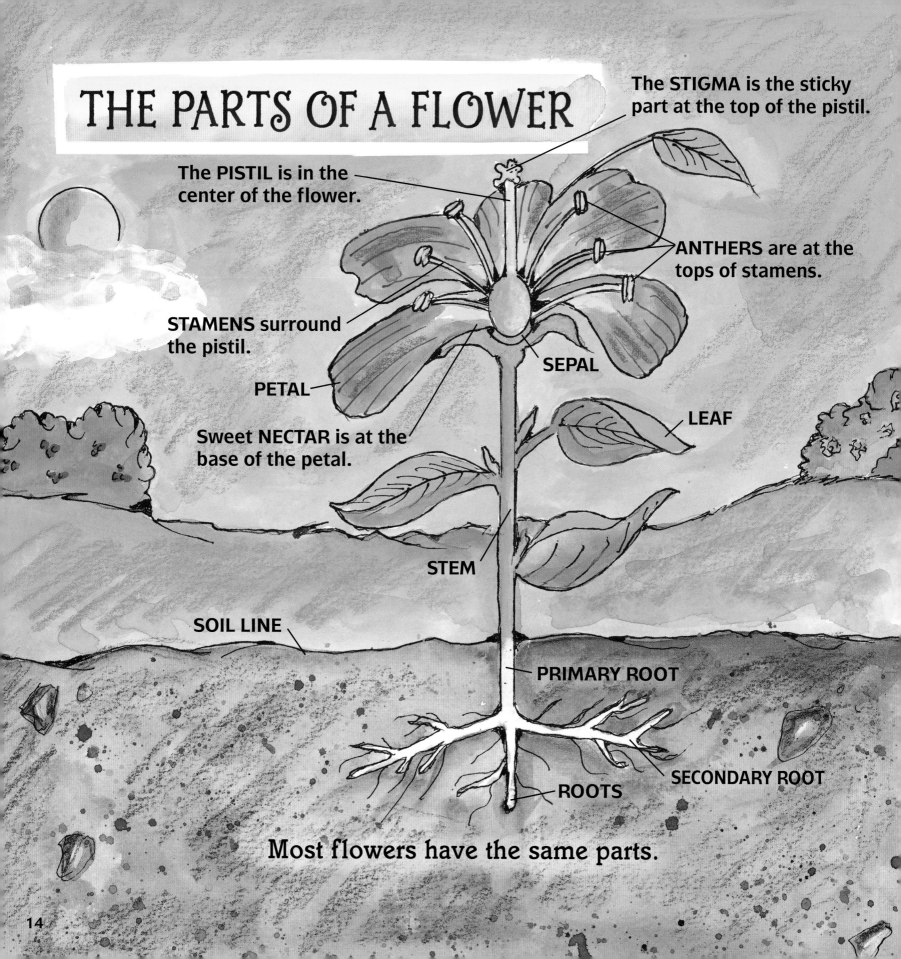

# THE PARTS OF A FLOWER

The STIGMA is the sticky part at the top of the pistil.

The PISTIL is in the center of the flower.

ANTHERS are at the tops of stamens.

STAMENS surround the pistil.

SEPAL

PETAL

Sweet NECTAR is at the base of the petal.

LEAF

STEM

SOIL LINE

PRIMARY ROOT

SECONDARY ROOT

ROOTS

Most flowers have the same parts.

# POLLINATION

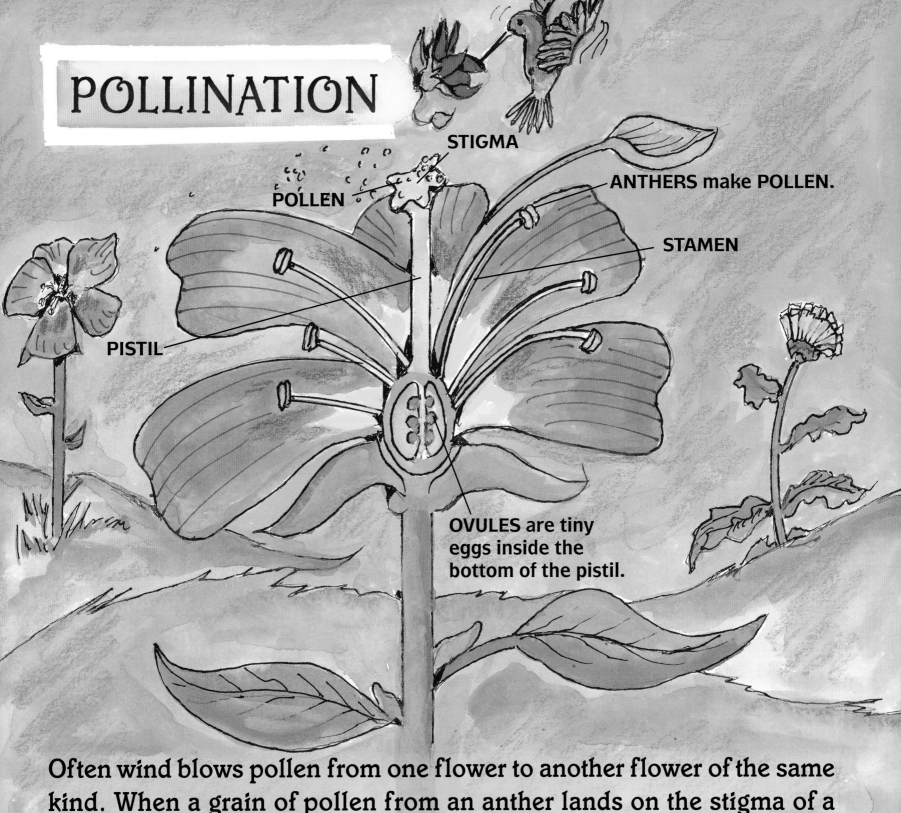

STIGMA

POLLEN

ANTHERS make POLLEN.

STAMEN

PISTIL

OVULES are tiny eggs inside the bottom of the pistil.

Often wind blows pollen from one flower to another flower of the same kind. When a grain of pollen from an anther lands on the stigma of a plant just like itself, pollination begins.

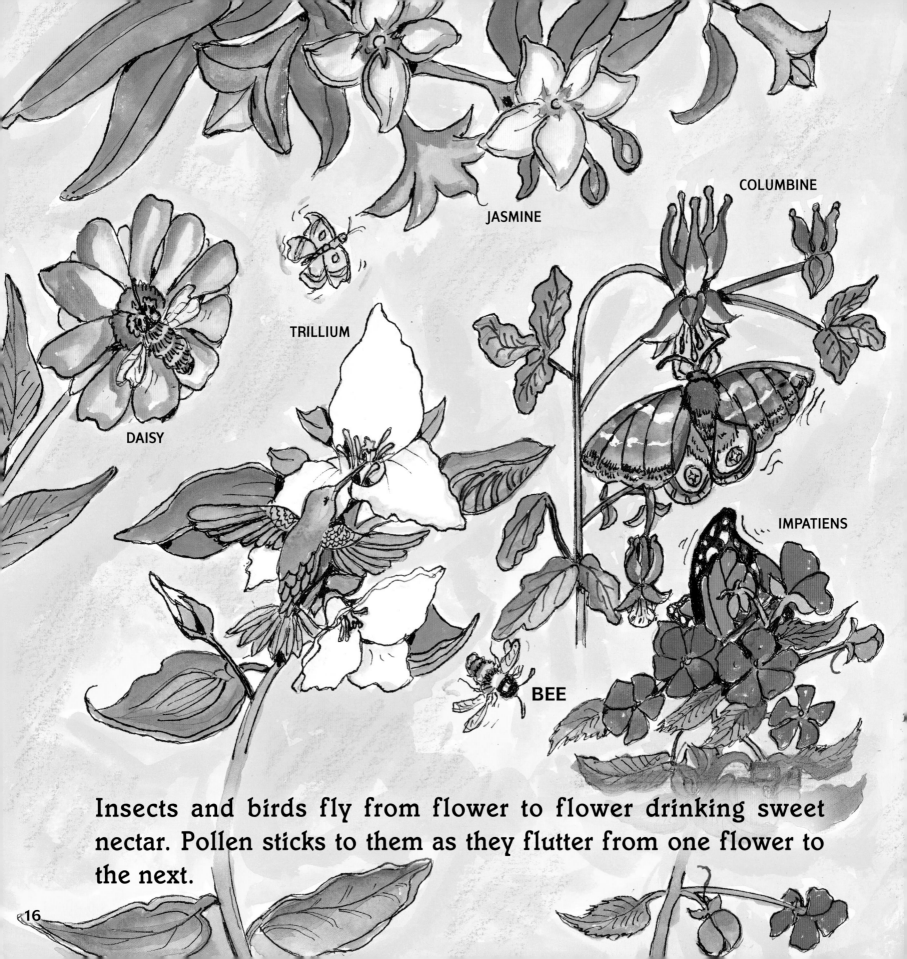

COLUMBINE

JASMINE

TRILLIUM

DAISY

IMPATIENS

BEE

Insects and birds fly from flower to flower drinking sweet nectar. Pollen sticks to them as they flutter from one flower to the next.

FUSCHIA

HUMMINGBIRD

BUTTERFLY

TULIPS

HOLLYHOCK

Pollinators are attracted to the bright colors and scents of the flowers.

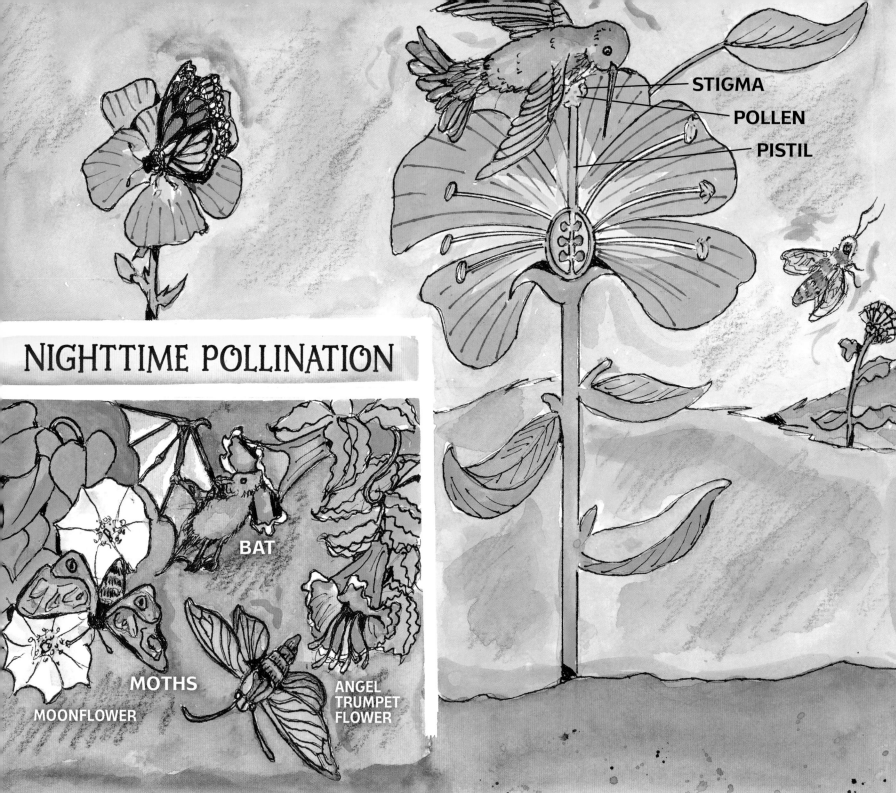

STIGMA

POLLEN

PISTIL

## NIGHTTIME POLLINATION

BAT

MOTHS

MOONFLOWER

ANGEL TRUMPET FLOWER

When pollinators fly to other flowers the pollen rubs off onto the sticky stigmas.

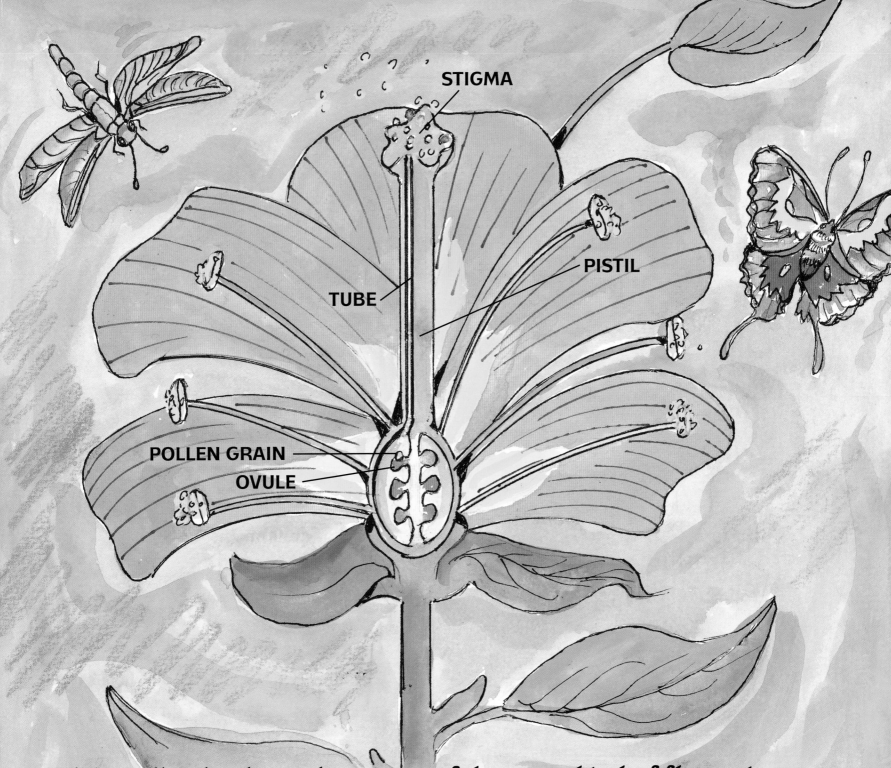

**STIGMA**

**PISTIL**

**TUBE**

**POLLEN GRAIN**

**OVULE**

When pollen lands on the stigma of the same kind of flower it came from, a long tube grows through the pistil. The pollen moves down the tube and fertilizes an ovule. A seed begins to grow.

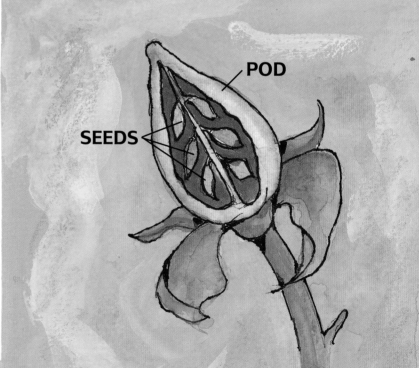

POD

SEEDS

Seeds grow inside the flower. As the flower dies the seeds get bigger. Often a pod grows around the seeds to protect them.

**APPLE**

SQUASH

Some seeds grow to become a fruit or vegetable we eat. Without pollination we wouldn't have fruits and vegetables.

# HOW SEEDS TRAVEL

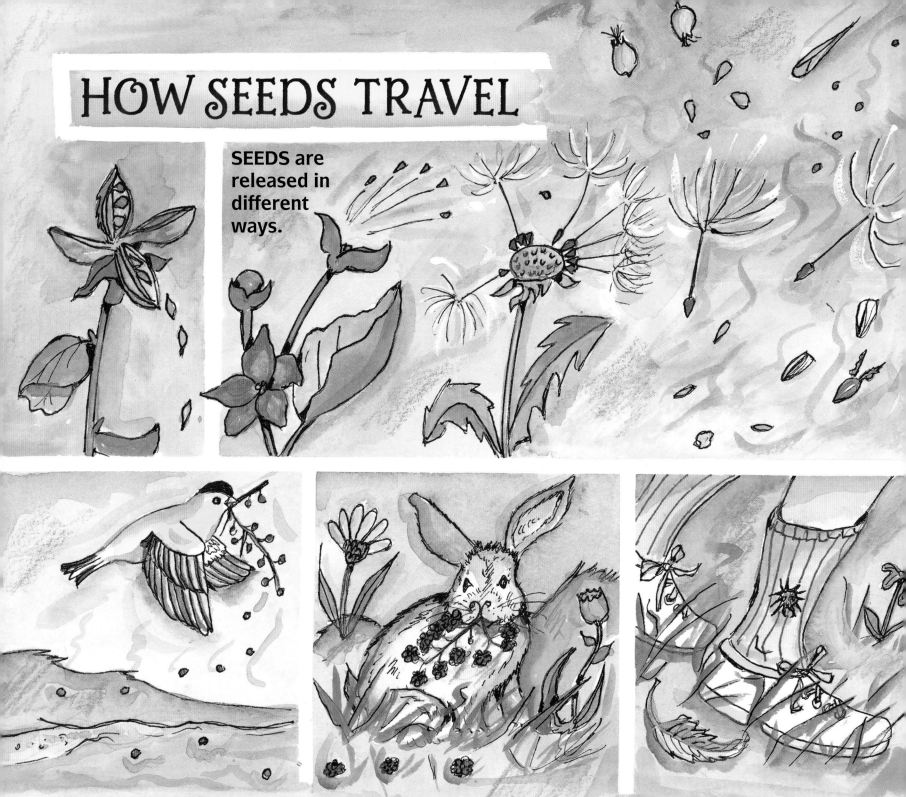

SEEDS are released in different ways.

When a flower pod ripens the seeds can fall out. The wind blows some seeds to the ground. Also, birds and animals move other seeds around.

The seeds travel to places where they can grow. Sometimes they have to wait until the next warm growing season.

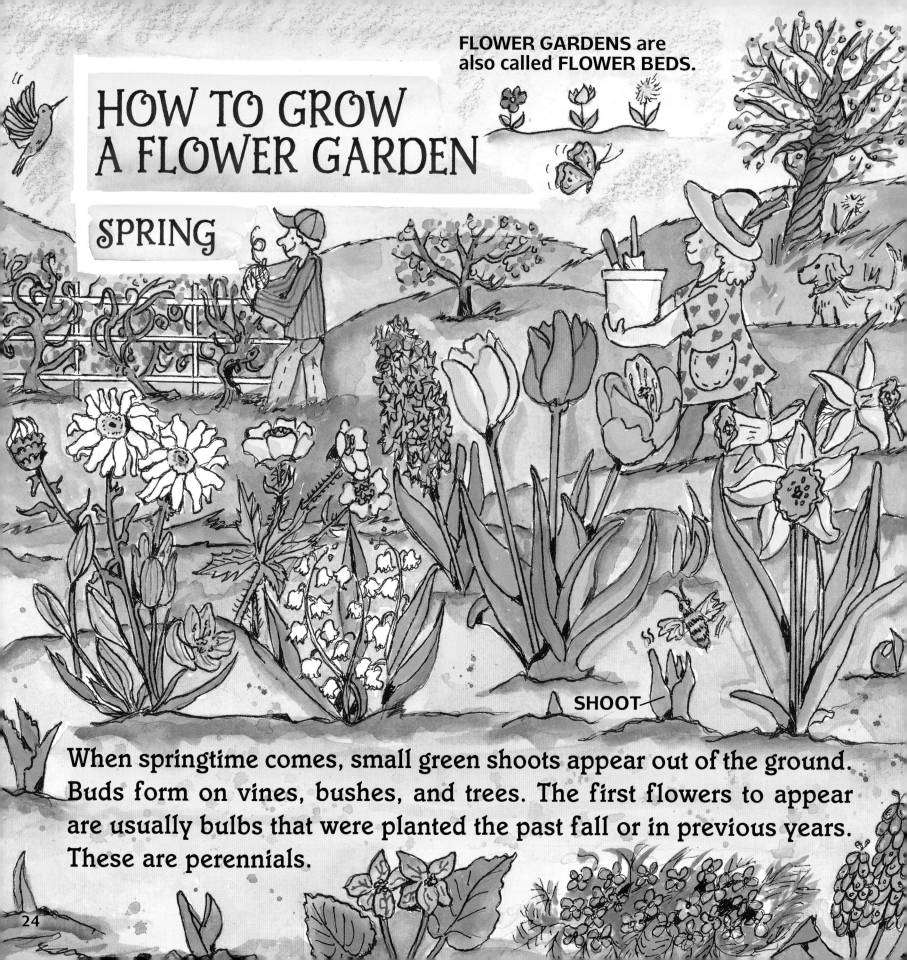

# HOW TO GROW A FLOWER GARDEN

## SPRING

FLOWER GARDENS are also called FLOWER BEDS.

SHOOT

When springtime comes, small green shoots appear out of the ground. Buds form on vines, bushes, and trees. The first flowers to appear are usually bulbs that were planted the past fall or in previous years. These are perennials.

ORGANIC FERTILIZERS and COMPOST are made up of broken-down leaves, grasses, and other waste, and are mixed into the soil.

SHOVEL

SPADE

RAKE

HOE

It's time to begin a new planting season. Clear the garden area and loosen up the soil. Plan the garden so each plant has enough room to grow.

SEEDLINGS

SEEDS

ASTERS

SUNFLOWER DAISY

SEED PACKETS

LUPINE

LILIES ASTERS ROSES BUSH

PERENNIAL PLANTS

Garden stores have seed packets and starter plants. Some people send away for seeds and plants. You can also choose full-grown plants to place in the ground or in containers.

VIOLET

WATERING
CAN

SUNFLOWER

HAND
TROWEL

HAND
CLAW
RAKE

WINDOW BOX

Follow the directions on how to plant your flower seeds. Place larger plants and seedlings into holes. Pack the soil around them. Be sure to water new plantings. It's fun to watch the springtime flowers grow.

SUMMER

SUNFLOWERS

WEEDING is important so flowers have room to grow.

SUPPORTS

SPRINKLER

HOSE

GLADIOLAS

FENCE

CLIMBING ROSES

TIGER LILIES

MORNING GLORIES

TRELLIS

WATERING CAN

DAHLIAS

ASTERS

The summer flowers blossom next.

BEGONIAS

MARIGOLDS

FALL

SQUASH

APPLES

MUMS

MARIGOLDS

ASTERS

At last, when fall comes all the autumn flowers bloom. Some people plant next year's bulbs. Before it gets too cold, harvest fruits and vegetables and bring potted flowers inside to enjoy! Cover your flower beds to protect them from the cold.

**GREENHOUSES** protect seedlings and plants from harsh weather.

People like to pick flowers from their garden for family and friends.

Some communities have gardens where people meet to plant flowers and care for them. Many schools plant flower gardens and grow flowers in their classrooms to study and enjoy.

FUCHSIA

GERANIUM

CARNATION

CACTUS    ORCHID

MARIGOLD        PANSY        DAISY        IRIS

For special occasions some people send flowers or go to florists to buy flowers for themselves or others. People love to enjoy flowers all year long!

# FLOWER FACTS

## BIRTHDAY FLOWERS

Find the flower for your birthday month.

The RAFFLESIA flower can be 3 feet (1 meter) wide and can weigh 15 pounds (7 kilograms).

**The two biggest flowers are RAFFLESIA and the TITAN ARUM. Both flowers smell awful to attract insects for pollination.**

The TITAN ARUM, also called the CORPSE FLOWER, can be 7 to 12 feet (2 to 3.5 meters) tall.

**Some flower scents are used to make fragrant-smelling soaps, candles, perfumes, and other products.**

**JANUARY**

CARNATION

**FEBRUARY**

VIOLET

**MARCH**

DAFFODIL

**APRIL**

DAISY

**MAY**

LILY OF THE VALLEY

**JUNE**

ROSE

**JULY**

WATER LILY

**AUGUST**

GLADIOLUS

**SEPTEMBER**

ASTER

**OCTOBER**

MARIGOLD

**NOVEMBER**

CHRYSANTHEMUM

**DECEMBER**

HOLLY

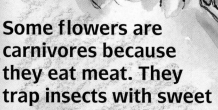

DEWY PINE

PITCHER PLANT

**Some flowers are carnivores because they eat meat. They trap insects with sweet scents, sticky surfaces, and parts that snap shut.**

VENUS FLYTRAP

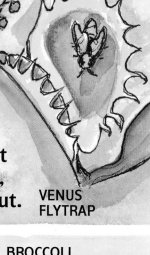

CAULIFLOWER

BROCCOLI

**We eat some flowers such as cauliflower, broccoli, and Brussels sprouts.**

BRUSSELS SPROUTS

BELLFLOWER

**Flowers follow the movement of the sun during the day.**

# Driving my Tractor

## Jan Dobbins & David Sim

**Barefoot Books**
*Celebrating Art and Story*

New Lenox
Public Library District
120 Veterans Parkway
New Lenox, Illinois 60451

Driving my tractor down a bumpy road,

And in my trailer, there's a heavy load.

There's a black-and-white cow
Going moo, moo, moo!
It's a very busy day.

Chug, chug,
Clank, clank, toot!

It's a very busy day.

Driving my tractor down a bumpy road,

And in my trailer, there's a heavy load.

There are two grey donkeys
Going eeyore, eeyore!
It's a very busy day.

Chug, chug,
Clank, clank, toot!

It's a very busy day.

Driving my tractor down a bumpy road,

And in my trailer, there's a heavy load.

There are three pink pigs
Going oink, oink, oink!

It's a very
busy day.

Chug, chug,
Clank, clank, toot!
It's a very busy day.

Driving my tractor down a bumpy road,

And in my trailer, there's a heavy load.

There are four white lambs
Going mah, mah, mah!
It's a very busy day.

Chug, chug,
Clank, clank, toot!

It's a very busy day.

Driving my tractor down a bumpy road,

And in my trailer, there's a heavy load.

There are five brown chickens
Going cluck, cluck, cluck!
It's a very busy day.

Chug, chug,
Clank, clank, toot!

It's a very busy day.

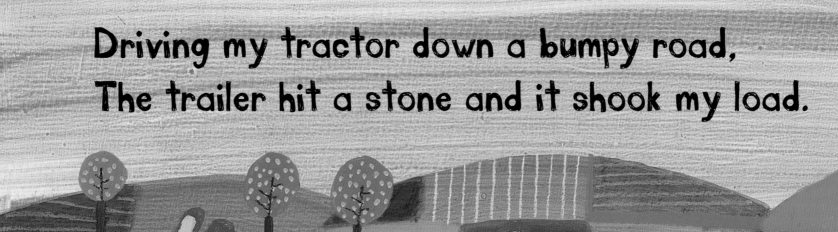

Driving my tractor down a bumpy road,
The trailer hit a stone and it shook my load.

The animals fell out, and they ran away!

It's a very busy day.

Driving my tractor back home again,
Chugging along down the bumpy lane,

# Farmers have lots of different machines to help them with their work.

Trailers carry foodstuffs, animals and other equipment.

Tractors tow heavy equipment, such as trailers and plows.

Plows turn the soil to make it ready for sowing seeds.

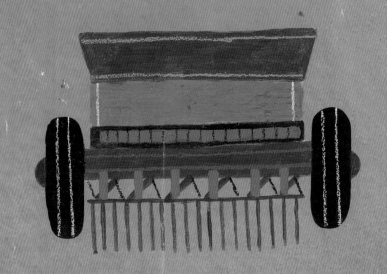

Seed drills plant seeds deep in the soil.

Combine harvesters cut wheat, oats and barley and separate the grain from the stems.

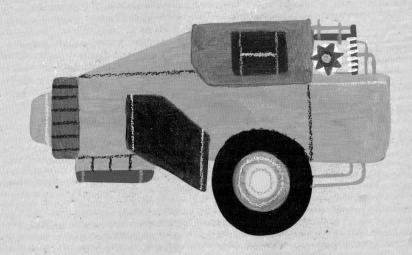

Balers gather harvested grain stems or mown grass and make them into bales of straw or hay.

Trucks transport smaller items than trailers and are designed to move easily across rough ground.

Milk trucks take milk from dairy farms to factories.

# These are some of the crops that farmers grow.

Potatoes and sweet potatoes are sown in spring and are ready to be harvested when they have flowered.

Carrots are grown from seeds. They can be cultivated nearly all year round.

Sunflowers can be grow during the summer.

Beetroot is sown in spring and harvested from summer to autumn.

Onions and leeks are planted in spring, and are usually ready to eat by mid-summer.

Wheat, barley and oats are cereal crops. They are usually sown in spring and harvested during late summer.

Squash and pumpkins are sown in late spring or early summer. They can be picked when quite young, or left to grow larger.

Sweet corn is a cereal crop. It is sown in spring.

Cabbages, cauliflower and turnips are usually sown in spring and harvested in summer or autumn. Cabbages are also grown in winter.

# Driving my Tractor

# Barefoot Books
## Celebrating Art and Story

At Barefoot Books, we celebrate art and story that opens
the hearts and minds of children from all walks of life, inspiring
them to read deeper, search further, and explore their own creative gifts.
Taking our inspiration from many different cultures, we focus on themes that
encourage independence of spirit, enthusiasm for learning, and sharing of
the world's diversity. Interactive, playful and beautiful, our products
combine the best of the present with the best of the past to
educate our children as the caretakers of tomorrow.

### Live Barefoot!
Join us at www.barefootbooks.com

W9-AQW-206

## Imperial

# N ARMS

### EGAN THREE
### EEKS AGO

LINI WAS TO SIGN
PITULATION

MADE THROUGH
N ARCHBISHOP

From MARTIN WORK

---

## NEWS CHRONICLE

# THE CROWNING GLORY:
# EVEREST IS CLIMBED

**THE QUEEN'S DRESS TODAY** Back Page

Tremendous news for the Queen

### HILLARY DOES IT

### WHO CARES NOW IF IT SNOWS?

---

## DAILY EXPRESS

SATURDAY OCTOBER 5 1957

### The first 'Flying Saucer' travels at 17,000 m.p.h.

# SPACE AGE IS HERE

## Soviet satellite circling world in 95 minutes

By CHAPMAN PINCHER

**Mrs. Mike Parker names woman**

### THAT 7%

WILSON: I've evidence leak was political

MACMILLAN: I'll act if you prove it

**Warsaw rioters stone police**

WHY, LOOK WHO'S HERE!

SATELLITE 'SIGNALS' TO BRITAIN

Relax with Mr Brandyman

a long, refreshing drink with ginger ale or soda

## MARTELL

---

## The Daily Telegraph
and Morning Post

24-PAGE PICTURE SUPPLEMENT

No 30,545 LONDON WEDNESDAY JUNE 3 1953

Printed in LONDON and MANCHESTER   Price 3d

Don't say Gin— Gordon's

# ELIZABETH II IS CROWNED

## SPLENDOUR IN ABBEY SEEN BY MILLIONS

## QUEEN 4 TIMES ON PALACE BALCONY: VAST CROWDS

## ROYAL BROADCAST: PLEDGE TO SERVICE OF HER PEOPLES

WITH THE SPLENDOUR AND SOLEMNITY OF AN HISTORIC RITUAL INSIDE WESTMINSTER ABBEY WITH TRADITIONAL POMP AND COLOUR AND PAGEANTRY ALONG THE ROYAL ROUTE OUTSIDE ELIZABETH II WAS YESTERDAY CROWNED QUEEN AMID THE AFFECTIONATE ACCLAIM OF MILLIONS OF HER PEOPLE IN THIS COUNTRY AND THROUGHOUT HER GREAT COMMONWEALTH OF NATIONS

# AFTER THE WAR WAS OVER

MICHAEL FOREMAN

FRANKLIN PIERCE
COLLEGE LIBRARY
RINDGE, N.H. 03461

Copyright © 1995 by Michael Foreman

All rights reserved. No part of this book may be
reproduced in any form or by any electronic or
mechanical means, including information storage
and retrieval systems, without permission in writing
from the publisher, except by a reviewer who may
quote brief passages in a review.

FIRST U.S. EDITION 1996

ISBN 1-55970-329-6
Library of Congress Catalog Card Number
95-83504
Library of Congress Cataloging-in-Publication
information is available.

Published in the United States by Arcade Publishing,
Inc., New York
Distributed by Little, Brown and Company

10 9 8 7 6 5 4 3 2 1

Designed by Janet James

PRINTED IN ITALY

CURR
PR
6056
.0675
Z463
1996

**TO OUR MUM**

who was always there

and

is always here

It was summer, 1945. The war was over. The victory bonfires blazed on the village green and the embers remained hot enough for days to bake potatoes. When the fires cooled, the ashes drifted and spiralled like silver-grey snow.

The victory flags stayed up for ages. More flags and bunting were added as the men began to return home to the village. Some took months to get back from the Far East, particularly if they had been badly wounded or had suffered in Japanese prisoner-of-war camps.

The pain felt by the children whose fathers would never return was made worse by the flags and 'Welcome Home' banners. The last man home was Sid, from a Japanese camp.

Sid swopped his army uniform for a bus conductor's outfit and thereafter drank hot tea from the saucer with all the other bus crews in my mother's shop.

When each man was demobilized from National Service he was a given a cheap, ill-fitting 'demob' suit. These suits lasted within families for generations. They were first worn only on Sundays and at funerals and weddings. Then eventually the trousers were worn beneath dungarees for work, and the jackets passed down through the sons.

Teenagers (who were not then invented) did not have their own fashions. Children's clothes were the same as adults' clothes, but in smaller sizes. Younger brothers had the cast-offs of bigger brothers, but cut-down to fit. Not until the mid 1950s, when the Teddy Boys created their unique outfits, did the younger generation begin to have their own fashions.

The shop was also our home and it stood with two other little houses on a triangular traffic island surrounded by three roads. It was at the end of the bus route from town, and after turning the buses around, the drivers and conductors had a five-minute break. Mum made tea for them in a great big pot.

Although the war was over, there were still lots of uniforms in and out of our shop. The American Forces were still around, particularly on Saturday nights.

5/- DEPOSIT AND PAY OFF.
Delivered when Paid For.

D.B. TWO- SUIT
FINE PIECE CLOTH
SEMI- WORSTED

In Birds-
eye, Dia- £7.7.0
g o n a l PRICES SLASHED
Stripe de-
s i g n s. 99'6
C o l o u r s:
Light, Dark Brown, Grey,
Blues. Perfectly tailored. 34
in. to 42 in chest. State chest,
waist, inside leg measure,
colour, design, second choice.

RADIO

are essential. Ideal for Bed-
Invalids, Private Listening,
inded Boys, &c. No Electricity,
tteries. Works anywhere. Ivory
e case, unbreakable. 4¼ in. x 2
3½ in. Perfect Present. Radio's
t value—plus 1/6 post & pakg. or
D. 1/- ext.
Refund if unsuitable or call.
NTROSE PRODUCTS (Dept. R.20),
623/7 Holloway Road, London, N.19.

Roy Rogers
OFFICIAL
Flash-Draw
HOLSTER OUTFIT
with Swivel Hip Firing Action
Genuine Cowhide
The FASTEST DRAW You Ever Saw
Roy Rogers
Flash-Draw HOLSTER

The local girls went dancing with them at the Palais de Danse, and when the Americans began to be posted home, many of the girls married them. With dreams of Hollywood shining in their eyes, they moved to isolated farm communities in the wind-blown Mid West or trailer homes on the outskirts of Texas oil towns.

The pretty sisters of some of my friends became American brides and each Christmas sent sad letters and bits of shiny Americana to their families. The twins, Arthur and Kenny, received silver six-shooters with buffalo heads carved on the handles. The rest of us boys were deeply jealous, and wished we had pretty sisters.

The landscape of war was slowly cleared. When the first small area of beach was opened up it was immediately packed with people. We children had never been on the beach before. Suddenly, there we all were.

Grannies and grandads, aunts and uncles, mums and dads, packed on to a tiny patch of beach, and beyond the wire, mile after mile of sands and shingle still stuffed with mines. Gradually the beach was cleared of mines and barbed wire.

Bren gun carriers with caterpillar tracks were used to transport the mine disposal men along the beach from the village. We used to get rides with them to the latest frontier wire, and imagine we were fighting our way across the Sahara with the Desert Rats. Then we would look through the deep slits in the blockhouse at the controlled explosions of the mines along the beach. There was a wrecked landing craft on the shore. After the mines were cleared the wreck became our pirate ship.

The final act of celebration for the end of the war was a great gathering of all the children from the area on 'The Oval' cricket ground on the foreshore below the cliffs of Lowestoft. Hundreds and hundreds of us stood in pouring rain holding bits of coloured card over our heads while the bands played.

At a given signal we had to turn the card over. Viewed from the cliffs above, where all the townspeople were gathered, the cards together formed the Union Jack and when turned over again they read 'God Save the King!' The cards went soggy and colours ran down our arms.

Back at school, it was a shock suddenly to have men as teachers. All through the war our teachers had been women, many of them rather ancient. Teaching became much louder and punishment swift and effective. However, the new young Headmaster, Mr Newson, was, I thought, a great improvement on the old Head. The retirement of the old Head also meant the end of the reign of terror of his fearsome wife who taught the top class.

One day, at school, we had a visit from a policeman. We assembled in the school hall and the policeman laid out a collection of mines on the floor. There were many shapes and sizes. We were told *never* to touch anything metal which we might find lying on the beach. It was hoped that the local beach was now completely clear, but mines could still be loose in the sea and might get washed up on the shore. The policeman then stood on a mine and the metal casing flew apart. We screamed and jumped in the air. Even the teachers gasped and closed their eyes.

Of course, the policeman's mines were harmless, empty cases, but what a shock! We would never touch a metal object found on the beach – or anywhere else for that matter.

Miss West and other teachers retired but the younger women teachers stayed on. Pat Palmer was my favourite. Sometimes she took us for P.T. When we were doing physical jerks, each time she raised her arms above her head her short, yellow jumper rose above her waist. The arc of bare flesh above her skirt was like the morning sun rising from a dark sea. It was a whole new dawn for me.

One day, Miss Palmer asked us to paint a picture of a highwayman. At the end of the session she held up my picture as a good example.

'That's not very good, Miss,' chirped one of the boys. 'The bushes are just scribbles.'

'That's what real artists do,' replied Miss Palmer. 'They don't draw every leaf. They give the *impression* of things.'

It seemed like an easy way out to me, and it was the first time I had heard of artists. Not a bad job if you can get away with scribbles.

*Note the turned-down wellies. I thought they made me look like a pirate.*

There was a lot of saluting of flags in those days. The big occasion was Empire Day. The whole school would assemble in the playground. Old Father Time, the caretaker, slowly and dramatically hoisted the Union Jack up the flagpole while we saluted. Then we would sing 'God Save the King', and 'Land of Hope and Glory' and various songs of Empire. After some prayers we went in to school and looked at the big map which showed most of the world coloured pink.

I assumed that pink was the colour of the Empire because British people were supposed to be pink. But I always thought it a soppy colour and in games of Cowboys and Indians always wanted to be the Indian brave, or Sabu the elephant boy.

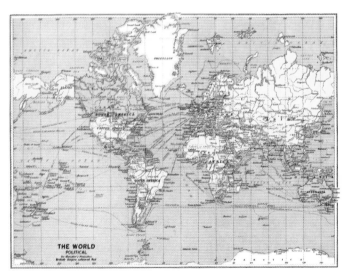

One night, just after the end of the war, my mother took us all to the Hippodrome, the local theatre.

She had often told us of a night before the war when she had gone to the Hippodrome to see Gracie Fields, 'Our Gracie'. That evening had kept our Mum and Aunt Louie in songs all through the war.

Now we were all going! I was so excited. There were lots of people on the stage at the beginning, singing and dancing in a line.

Then a lady came on in a spectacular red dress and lots of fruit on her head. She was singing and shaking about, then she took off her dress. Then her stockings. When her hands went behind her back to take off her bra, I pretended I had dropped something on the floor and ducked under my seat. I was too embarrassed to be looking at all this while sitting next to my mother.

Of course, I continued to peep from under my seat.

Suddenly the bra was off and two tennis balls dropped out, and the man (for it was an all-man show) danced off the stage, bouncing the balls. What a relief. The show was called *Soldiers In Skirts*.

Bomb sites continued to be our adventure playgrounds. Marigolds and potatoes grew in the ruins of buildings, and blitzed gardens offered apples and pears. Of course, we ate them long before they were ripe.

Some of my friends who had been bombed out of their homes were living in ex-Army huts. Geoffrey Dann, who had curly ginger hair and freckles, lived in one and I rather envied his new home with its great curved iron roof like an aircraft hangar.

R.B.1
16

MINISTRY OF
FOOD
1953-1954

MF

SERIAL N°

BE 130

RATION BOOK

Surname MACE GLYAN A Initials
Address 44 FLORENCE Rd
PAKEFIELD
LOWESTOFT

IF FOUND
RETURN TO
ANY FOOD
OFFICE

F.O. CODE No.

E—E
2

*Pre-fabricated houses (prefabs) were quickly built – more than 40,000 between 1945 and 1946.*

*The rationing of wartime continued long into the peace Bread and potatoes for a year or two, and butter, cheese, bacon, meat, tea and sugar were all rationed until 1954. Sweets were unrationed, at last, in April 1951. But so much was instantly gobbled up that rationing was re-introduced in July.*

The large gun emplacements dotted along the clifftops remained for years after the war. The 'pillboxes' and network of underground concrete tunnels can still be found beneath dense tangles of brambles and nettles.

Puggy Utton, a local hermit, lived in a pillbox and some of the connecting tunnels for years. He wore all his clothes at once: several coats, a hat over a balaclava, and through the holes in his gloves could be seen more gloves.

The clifftop setting, and the fear of suddenly bumping into the mysterious Puggy in the dark tunnels, made it a favourite playground for us boys. They were smelly places, often ankle deep in water, and we would frighten ourselves with ghostly moans and screams.

A few yards back from the cliff edge were fields of turnips, peas and potatoes. We helped ourselves to the occasional turnip and handful of potatoes, chipped them up with Squirt's fireman's axe and boiled them in a tin can for dinner. Squirt, being a fireman's son, always had a small axe and a box of matches.

We were often away from home the whole day, roaming free like a band of Indians. Parents in those days had less reason to worry about the whereabouts of their children. Everyone in the village knew everyone else. The roads were not full of strangers in cars.

The cliff path in spring and summer buzzed and
shimmered with bugs and beetles and chirruping
grasshoppers. There were butterflies in great numbers:
Red Admirals, Painted Ladies, Orange Tips, Clouded
Yellows, spectacular Peacocks and the modest
Common Blue. I thought it was the most *uncommon*
blue. A drop of the blue Mediterranean against the
grey-brown of the North Sea.

There were lacewings and stoneflies, and dragonflies
like green camouflaged bombers. As we lay in the grass,
we were dive-bombed by hornets and sawflies, digger
wasps and bees. Red ants and black ants surrounded
and attacked us like Lilliputian armies.

If we leaned over the cliff edge we could see, just
out of reach, Sand Martins constantly landing and taking
off from their vertical airfield, the cliff face riddled with
their nesting holes.

The cliff path wound through head-high hogweed
and cow parsley. There was dockweed which we used
to spit on and press on nettle stings to ease the pain. (I
thought they were called 'Doc' because it was short for
doctor.) May blossom hid thorns which could rip both
shirt and shoulder, and nettles stung bare legs as we
whooped and galloped our imaginary Indian ponies
through the sage brush.

COMMON BLUE.

WILLS'S CIGARETTES.

WILLS'S CIGARETTES.

PURPLE EMPEROR.

25

In late summer, corn and poppies were laid low by harvesters and surprised blue-eyed periwinkles blinked from the fields of stubble.

We didn't appreciate the beauty of such things then. We noticed them only when our bunch of harebells, buttercups and field forget-me-nots and wild honeysuckle handed to our mums might soften our late tea-time return.

*Vinca minor*

PERIWINKLE

Family RANUNCULACEÆ

BUTTERCUP

Family BORAGINACEÆ

FORGET-ME-NOT

*Lonicera Periclymenum*

HONEYSUCKLE

Family PAPAVERACEÆ

RED POPPY

Family CAMPANULACEÆ

BELLFLOWER

Against this background of beauty, we sometimes found horror. Farmers were angered by rabbits eating their crops and introduced a disease called myxomatosis which spread through the rabbit population with great speed and with terrible results.

Often, we would turn a bend in the path and find a rabbit crouched before us. Normally, rabbits would bound away to safety, but the diseased rabbits did not move. They stared with accusing, bulging eyes in pitifully swollen heads, ears flat along quivering bodies until they died.

We were brutal little boys, and had in the past chased rabbits in the hope of getting one for the pot. But the suffering of the diseased rabbits sickened us. Even our dogs seemed horrified, and whimpered and peered at the rabbits from behind our legs.

One day, two strange boys arrived at school. One was very tall, the other had a very round face and startling white hair. The strangest thing about them was their trousers, which were incredibly short. We Pakefield boys had the usual very baggy British knee-length trousers which made the backs of your legs sore in cold, wet weather, and long grey socks which always slipped down around our ankles. These strange boys had tight trousers, hardly lower than their bums, and bright white ankle socks.

The tall boy was called Henno, and the other Rigo. They were from Estonia, and stood in the bleak playground with their backs against the wall. Their knees looked very cold. Being British children, we teased them. Maybe children everywhere are like that if they are in a crowd.

But there was something about the two strange boys which excited me. They had come from somewhere else. They had seen things we hadn't. They were refugees.

Henno and Rigo walked past our shop every morning on their way to school. I would watch for them and walk out of the shop just as they were passing and wander along to school with them. They knew little English in the beginning and so of course spoke mostly to each other as we walked. I learned that Rigo's father was captain of a cargo ship and had managed to bring Rigo and Henno and their mothers out of Estonia before the Russians made it impossible.

After a short time, Henno and his mother moved on to Canada, and Rigo and I became close friends.

Rigo's father was sailing all over the world, and Rigo and his mother lived in a flat decorated by the paintings his father did during his long voyages. I thought the paintings were brilliant. They were always of the sea, often of a small sailboat with a man, a woman and a small boy with startling white hair at the tiller.

One day Rigo and I picked blackberries together on 'Sixteen Acre', an area of thick bushes bordering on the cliffs. I gave Rigo an empty jam jar to put his blackberries in. He asked me what it was called. I said, 'a jam jar'. He fell about laughing. 'Jam jar' were the funniest words he had ever heard. He repeated them all afternoon. 'Jam jar. Jam jar. Jam jar.'

Eventually he too moved on to live in Canada. I never heard from him again. He had taught me how to count up to twenty in Estonian, and I had taught him to say 'jam jar'. Wherever he is, I hope he has a sailboat and children with startling white hair.

Shortly after the war my mother took me to London on the train. We had free tickets because my father worked on the railway before he died. He died one month before I was born. We went to see Buckingham Palace.

Buckingham Palace was disappointing because it didn't have towers and turrets and didn't look like a palace. The guards outside still wore their khaki wartime uniforms and not red tunics and busby helmets.

Next day, we had a picnic in Hyde Park. The parks of London were still full of sheep from the wartime and the sheep got most of our picnic. In the afternoon we went to Whiteley's, a big department store which was much more like a palace. Mum bought me two model soldiers. They each cost half a crown (12$\frac{1}{2}$ pence in today's money), an enormous sum, I thought. One of them, an eighteenth-century infantryman, I still have, minus his head. It is the only toy which remains from my childhood.

I remember on my birthday a couple of years later getting a set of soldiers from an aunt. A complete set. A dozen all lined up in a box. Red tunics and busbies. I was thrilled. My mother said my aunt shouldn't have spent so much money and I was too old for such things. Too old. I could feel the lights going out on my childhood.

I grew up on a diet of comics and magazines. As my mother ran the village shop, we sold almost everything, including Sunday newspapers. The comics and magazines arrived in our shop on Wednesdays, to be delivered on Sundays. This meant I could read all the comics and as many magazines as I wanted before they were delivered.

One of my favourite comics was *Film Fun* which had real film stars in the comic strips and was printed in black and white. Laurel and Hardy were always on the cover and usually ended up having a huge meal of bangers and mash on a silver dish. I also liked Desperate Dan in *The Dandy*, who ran through brick walls to get to his enormous helpings of cow-pie. Perhaps I was attracted to these stories because of food rationing.

I also liked *The Wizard, Hotspur* and *Rover,* with their longer stories of heroic boys and dogs and secret agents. Later, a new comic, *Eagle,* appeared but I didn't like it. It was not daft enough.

Some of the magazines, particularly *John Bull,* used lots of drawings. One artist specialized in wonderful crowd scenes. Crowds at race meetings, railway stations, football matches. I remember his surname was Rose, and I wish I knew more about him.

In those days biscuits were not packed in small packets as they are now. They were delivered to the shop in large tins and customers would buy half a pound or so and Mum would weigh them out into paper bags or wrap them in old newspaper. The big biscuit tins were lined with white corrugated paper and each layer of biscuits was separated by transparent greaseproof paper. The white corrugated paper was smooth on one side. I used to draw crowd scenes on the smooth side and used the greaseproof as tracing paper. The biscuit tins were about twelve inches square, so unfolded, the paper for my crowds would be four feet long.

*I used to lie on the floor in front of the fire and draw for hours. We had the* Daily Mirror *for the news and the* Daily Express *because I liked to copy Rupert.*

*I used to copy drawings of Jane and throw them on the fire before my mother saw them.*

*I loved stories of space travel and never thought it would happen in my lifetime.*

### Rupert and the Jumping Men—30

A moment later the tiny airplane has landed and Rupert runs forward as an old friend gets out of it. "Why, surely you're the Golliwog that runs errands for like Rupert of Nutwood but you're four sizes too small!" "Yes, I am Rupert," says the little bear. "I couldn't get in here while I was my right size." And he tells

33

"NEWFOOTY"
TABLE SOCCER
Patent No. 638860.
ASSOCIATION FOOTBALL
FROM FIELD TO TABLE
Played with 22 miniature men, ball
and goals. F.A. Rules adapted.
★ THE ORIGINAL GAME with
LATEST IMPROVEMENTS! ★
★ FULL OF SOCCER THRILLS
★ FOULS OFFSIDE PENALTIES
★ RESULTS DEPEND UPON SKILL
ONLY "NEWFOOTY" HAS 100%
SELF-RIGHTING PATENT MEN.

Played
Throughout
British Isles
and Abroad.

BUY THE
ORIGINAL!

Prices, 10/11, 14/11 and 18/11 POST
FREE, or send 2d stamp for details.
THE "NEWFOOTY" CO., Dept. T,
RICE LANE, LIVERPOOL, 9.
BUY NOW FOR XMAS!

My brothers, my friends and I delivered the Sunday papers. I used to walk my paper round, kicking a tennis ball along the roads, lanes and back alleys. I was becoming football mad.

For Christmas one year I was given a table football set, and after they had delivered the papers, some of the paper boys used to stay behind and we would have a table football competition in our front room and imitate the roar of the crowd.

We played football at school, and every weekend except in the cricket season. Then in the cricket season, when the evenings were long and light, we played football every weekend *and* every evening. We also played a special version of football on the concrete road by the Green. With two players on each team it was rather like foot-tennis. 'Tap Tin', our version of 'Kick the Can', conkers, hoops, kites, fishing and the making of buggies from old prams and fish boxes, filled our days to bursting.

Girls didn't feature much in our lives. We sat next to them at school, some of my friends had them as sisters, but in general they were as popular as nettles and best avoided.

Two or three girls, however, were exceptions. They used to hover around the edge of our games and occasionally join in. The girls would try to give the ball a few hefty kicks, then invariably grab the ball and run off with it. We would give chase and the football match would degenerate into a game of rugby with us all in a heap. Sometimes I was fed up because our game had been ruined, but sometimes I found it more fun than football.

Then, one day, the ladies who worked at the local laundry decided to form a rugby team to play in a charity game. I don't remember who their opponents were going to be, but the laundry wanted to play a practice match against us boys – so they could get accustomed to the rules.

*Many of the ladies were enormous and none of them bothered with the rules. They thought the game was about sitting on as many small boys as possible.*

Just across the road at the back of our house was the fish and chip shop. It was the favourite place to hang about in the evenings. It had a wide pavement in front, and the light, which streamed from its big steamed-up window, was bright enough to read comics by.

The owner of the chip shop was Lofty Payne. He was sports mad and on Saturdays he often took me to Norwich in his fish van to see the football. By the time I arrived home, brother Pud would have finished his bath in front of the kitchen fire and emptied it with the bucket and gone off to meet his girlfriend, Doreen.

Usually, my big brother Ivan was in the bath, having refilled it from the kettle. I would sit at the kitchen table beside the bath and have my tea and give him a full report of the match.

If I didn't go to a match, we would listen to 'Sports Report' – Ivan in the bath and me at the tea table, checking his football coupon. Then Ivan would get out, dress in his Saturday night suit, and go to the Palais de Danse. I would then get in the bath and finish my tea.

When I eat celery I always think of those Saturday nights. I don't know if it is because I always ate celery then or whether sticks of celery remind me of Ivan's legs. The tin bath, though big for me, was far too small for Ivan. He had to be a contortionist to scrub all his bits and pieces.

Mum and Aunt Louie were still busy in the shop. I would tip out half the bath water and top it up with boiling water ready for Mum. Mum closed the shop at 7.30 on Saturdays so she could be in the bath to listen to 'Saturday Night Theatre' while Louie took the dog for a walk.

Later, I discovered the jazz programme on A.F.N. (American Forces Network). This became my bathtime listening. It was the era of the big, roaring be-bop bands and was so exciting. Sometimes I pretended my lemonade bottle was a trumpet and mimed to the mirror, standing in the bath in front of the fire.

Our dog was called Sandy. We got him as a tiny puppy in the winter of 1947, the worst winter of the century. Deep snow stayed for weeks. Little could move on the roads, and the railways were at a standstill. Some power stations ran out of coal, and electricity was turned off several times a day. Farmers could not plough their fields so the following harvest was poor.

*Mum, me and Sandy.*

Of course, we boys loved the snow, but it was difficult for a tiny puppy like Sandy. He was too small to walk through the deep snow, so he jumped into and out of my footprints wherever we went.

Spring brought gales and floods. By 1948 rations were lower than during the war. The general feeling was that things could only get better. Very young children were given free orange juice, cod liver oil (yuk) and tonics and vitamins. Free milk was provided for all children at school until Mrs Thatcher the Milk Snatcher took it away from all children over seven in 1971.

Although many men had returned home from the Army, Navy and Air Force, many younger men were being 'called up' to take their places and maintain the 'Peace' around the world. Eighteen-year-olds were required for a compulsory period of two years' military service, so that if war broke out again Britain would have a large number of trained young men ready to fight.

Lowestoft station, like railway stations throughout the country, continued to be a place of sad farewells. Dads were home at last, but now elder brothers were in uniform and going away.

Trouble started in Palestine. Jews and Arabs were killing each other and both sides were killing the British.

Ivan was called up and sent to Egypt. We were all terribly sad to see him go, but his girlfriend Barbara, 'B', took me to the pictures every Thursday evening because she didn't like going alone.

We saw all kinds of films. Whatever was showing, we went. In addition to the main feature there would be the B film, usually a black-and-white drama. Then a cartoon or two, and the 'trailers' of forthcoming films, which always looked absolutely fantastic and the 'best film ever'. Then there would be a travelogue or short, factual film about making golf balls or knitting sweaters in the Hebrides. Sometimes there would be a singer on stage singing posh songs. Sometimes a man in a bow tie and a lady in a big frock would sing soppy songs. There would then be ice-creams and fruit drinks, and then everyone would settle back in the dense cigarette smoke, for the main feature.

'B' liked lovey-dovey films with lots of music and kissing. Once she took me out of the cinema because she was horrified by a film about war. She thought it unsuitable for me and it probably made her even more worried about Ivan.

I didn't like Saturday morning pictures with all the singing or the films made specially for kids. My mates and I went on Saturday afternoons to the real films. Hopalong Cassidy, who didn't sing, and best of all, Gabby Hayes, like a Wild West Father Christmas. Roy Rogers and Gene Autry always burst into song and we booed them. We loved all things American. All our movie heroes – cowboys, Indians, even Robin Hood and his merry men – had American accents.

*My favourite films were pirate films because there was always a feast where they ate all kinds of exotic fruit, had bad table manners and a good time.*

Then, out of the steam and gloom of evening, Ivan's tall shape appeared with a kitbag across his shoulders.

In his kitbag were treasures from the East, as exotic as any pirate film. Sugared almonds. Dates with nuts inside. And a bedspread with camels, palm trees and pyramids for Mum. I don't know what he brought 'B' but they stopped going out together soon after.

Ivan wrote to us and sent the occasional photograph of himself and his mates standing outside tents with the pyramids far away in the distance. Eventually we got news of his return date.

I was at the Lowestoft railway station early in the morning. We had the date but not the time of his arrival. Train after train arrived. 'B' popped in to the station during her lunch break, but no sign of Ivan.

By my tenth birthday, Mum decided it was time I had a bike. All my friends had bikes. Mum was surprised I had not pestered her for one before. She didn't know I was scared of learning to ride.

It wasn't a new bike but it had a new coat of paint and was very smart and shiny. Despite the efforts of my brothers, their girlfriends and Aunt Louie, all of whom took turns running alongside the bike holding the saddle, I fell off every time they let go.

I made excuses not to ride. I said the bike was too big. Mum had wooden blocks screwed to the pedals so I could reach them more easily, but still I refused to learn. It was pointed out to me that next year I would have to go to secondary school which would be a long way to walk. 'Well, I'll learn *then*,' I said.

At about the same time, I started going to see the football at Norwich with some of the older newspaper boys. We went on the train.

Much as I loved the thrill of football, my fondest memories are of the journey there and back, and the companionship of older boys. The steam train rattled through the flat marshland of Norfolk, casting smuts over bullrushed dykes and the sails of windmills and boats on the wide broads.

The crowds in the late 1940s and 1950s were enormous. Even Third Division teams like Norwich regularly attracted crowds of 30,000. The supporters packed so tightly together that it was impossible to move. Boys were passed hand to hand over the heads of the crowd to the front so they could see. On one awful occasion someone behind me peed in my pocket. Probably a Millwall supporter.

Even the top footballers were paid very little. There was a maximum wage for all footballers and even Tommy Lawton, the top striker of his generation, could not earn more.

Here is the balance sheet of Tommy Lawton's eighteen years in the game.

| | £ | s. | d. |
|---|---|---|---|
| 40 winter weeks and 12 summer weeks at the limit for 17-year-olds | 352 | 0 | 0 |
| 40 winter and 12 summer weeks at the limit for 18-year-olds | 456 | 0 | 0 |
| 40 winter and 12 summer weeks at the limit for 19-year-olds | 580 | 0 | 0 |
| 15 seasons on top money: | | | |
| 600 winter weeks at £15 per week | 9,000 | 0 | 0 |
| 180 summer weeks at £12 per week | 2,160 | 0 | 0 |
| 3 benefits of £750 each | 2,250 | 0 | 0 |
| 1 accrued share of benefit (three-fifths) | 450 | 0 | 0 |
| 18 seasons' bonus at £1 a point (average, say, 42 points per season) | 756 | 0 | 0 |
| TOTAL | £16,004 | 0 | 0 |

In 1947, Denis Compton was named 'Sportsman of the Year'. He was every boy's hero because he played cricket for England and football for Arsenal and England. His face was on huge posters advertising Brylcreem. He was a dashing winger for Arsenal when they won the FA Cup in 1950. They wore gold shirts that day, and Denis looked even more glamorous than usual. His brother, Leslie, was centre half, and also kept wicket for Middlesex.

I can still name every member of that Arsenal team, as I can the Norwich team of that era, but I cannot name all the players of any team since.

On the side of our house was a large billboard. The posters were usually about the latest film, but sometimes there would be a giant Denis Compton smiling down above our loo.

Opposite our house, behind a row of old petrol pumps, was an even more gigantic poster of a golfer with a box of Swan Vesta matches. The two giant faces beamed at each other across the road, and in the tiny hut beside the petrol pumps Ginger Jarvis practised his trumpet, his feet sticking out through the window.

By now, Ivan and Pud were both working in the same garage in the town. Ivan was five years older than Pud, and Pud was nine years older than me. So we each had our own group of friends. I liked being with their friends – but they weren't very interested in mine.

Ivan's group all had motorbikes, and they rode around in a pack, but they couldn't be described as a motorcycle gang. In those days nobody had the flashy leather outfits bikers wear today. They didn't even have crash helmets. Just a pair of goggles, and perhaps a scarf to make them look more dashing.

Sometimes Ivan took me on the back of his bike. It was thrilling to roar along country lanes in a swarm of motorbikes and a cloud of blue smoke.

One weekend, cousin Pam came from London with a couple of girlfriends to watch their favourite speedway team, Wembley Lions, ride at Norwich. They spent Saturday with us on Pakefield beach, and Pud took them out in his boat.

It was quite a rough day, and when coming in to the shore, the boat slewed side-on to a big breaking wave and tipped everyone into the sea. The wave rolled them all up on to the beach in a tangle of arms, oars and legs, and to cheers from the local fishermen.

The three girls went to the speedway in the evening in an odd assortment of clothes borrowed from Mum and Aunt Louie. They took me with them and I was thrilled to see the legendary Tommy Price ride for Wembley. He had ridden for England many times before and after the war, and had a reputation for being a rough rider. He was booed by the Norwich fans and cheered wildly by Pam and her friends.

My favourite rider was Billy Bales. He was a local boy, and had started as a youngster on the cycle speedway track outside the stadium at Yarmouth. He was so good that he was invited to have a go on a proper speedway bike. He rode for Yarmouth Bloaters for a short time before becoming a First Division star at Norwich. The local girls loved him and the boys idolized him.

The World Champion at that time was an Australian, Jack Young, who rode for West Ham. He had great classic style, not at all like the hell-for-leather tear-aways like Tommy Price or the flashy Split Waterman.

When I went to Norwich with my mates, we always went first to the football. Then we had chips at the cattle market at the foot of Norwich Castle, before catching the bus to the speedway. On waste ground outside the stadium was the cycle speedway track – an oval scraped out of the turf and covered with cinders.

Local boys hurtled round this wearing the colours of their favourite teams. There were lots of crashes and it was always exciting. Most of the boys emulated the tactics of Tommy Price and rode their opponents off the track and into the straw bales, but they dreamed of being Billy Bales, local hero and Speedway International.

Billy Bales

After watching the cycle speedway, we had more chips, then went into the stadium. By now it was getting dark. The bright grass-green oval in the centre with the freshly painted white line around it, glowed like an atoll in a sea of volcanic ash. Men in white overalls raked the ash flat. Then with a roar of engines and the delicious smell of racing fuel, four riders came on to the track. Their helmets were brightly coloured, on their chests were emblazoned the Star of Norwich, or the rampant Lion of Wembley, or the Crossed Hammers of West Ham. Their leathers and machines shone like armour.

Suddenly, the starting tape flew up and the four riders raced at full speed into the first corner. Here the race was usually won or lost. The rider who got to the inside of the bend first stood the best chance of winning. The first bend was where most accidents occurred. If the inside man was going too fast and lost control of his bike he could take all the others into the fence, where they would lie spreadeagled, like knights of old, in a cloud of dust, with spinning wheels and broken bones.

Despite being such a speedway fan and admirer of the young cycle speedway racers, I was still too chicken to learn to ride my bike.

The bike remained under a potato sack amongst crates of vegetables in our tiny back yard.

THE SPIDER OF THE SPEEDWAYS

⊞▲▲▲▲▲▲▲▲▲▲▲▲▲▲▲▲▲▲▲⊞
**TROUBLE FOR SHENTON.**
⊞▼▼▼▼▼▼▼▼▼▼▼▼▼▼▼▼▼▼▼⊞
JIM (ROCKET) RADFORD of Bromchurch Tigers speedway club could not get Mac Shenton's warning out of his mi...
Mac...

There was a practice for the Saturday's return match against Norburn at Norburn, and the team was chosen. Rocket Radford was ...

about speedway racing and about who owned the clubs."

Tom Urzetti's hands tightened ...which he was

The Foreman brothers.

*Note the wreckage of war on the cliff face, and the gun emplacement top right.*

Pud was not interested in motorbikes. He was always drawn to the sea. He and his mates built canoes from thin strips of wood and canvas. They were rather pointy and angular, not like the streamlined fibreglass canoes of today.

One day, Pud allowed me to have a go in his canoe. As a precaution he tied a long rope to the bow so I wouldn't drift too far out to sea. I paddled around for a while but when I turned towards the shore the canoe tipped over. My legs were stuck and I couldn't get out. However, I could bend my head up between my knees into the belly of the canoe where there was an air pocket, and breathe. I was aware of several people frantically splashing around me in the water for what seemed like ages.

Then suddenly the canoe was tipped the right way up and I saw Pud's shocked face. He thought he had drowned me. The last place he expected to find me was still in the canoe.

The sea was the life blood of the town and the fish market was its heart. It was the scene of unbelievable activity as herring drifters steamed and jostled for position in the crowded harbour. Baskets of fish were hauled, dripping, from the decks of the drifters, and swung across the quay and tipped into boxes. Sunlight danced across the waters of the harbour, the gleaming fish, ice and yellow waterproofs of the men. Fish scales sequined every surface. Scottish fisher-girls, who followed the shoals of herring around the coast, gutted and packed fish by the million.

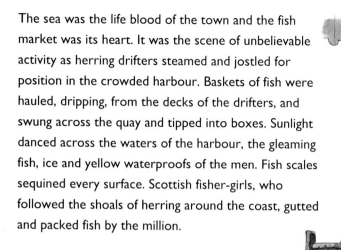

Tragedy was never far from the lives of the fishermen. Several boats were lost over the years. When one sank and three members of one family were drowned (a father and two sons) we crouched under the window of the house to see if we could hear crying. It was as quiet as the grave.

We boys were at the pierhead to see the *Lord Hood* land the biggest ever single catch of herrings: 314¾ crans (the weight of herring is measured in crans and this quantity was equal to about 56,000 kilograms). It was feared that the weight of the catch would be too much for the vessel in the strong swell.

I was still sleeping in my mother's room, but when Pud was twenty he had to do his National Service so he married his girlfriend, Doreen, before he went. Then Ivan married his new girl, Helen, and I got their room. The brothers had slept in the big bed all their lives. Under the bed was a chamber pot, and on a little marble-topped table was a jug and basin which rattled when you walked on the cold lino floor. There was a china chicken on a china nest hatching a bar of soap.

The teacher of the top class at Pakefield Primary School was Oscar Outlaw – a big man who must have been an officer in the war. He had an air of authority which none of us would dream of challenging.

He realized that none of us had books at home. It wasn't just because of the shortage of books due to the war – we came from a culture which had no books.

Oscar Outlaw decided to rectify this by reading from his own favourite boyhood books. One day he started reading *Treasure Island*. For me the two most magical words in English Literature are 'Treasure Island'. Just to hear those words today gives me the same tingle I felt when I was first introduced to Jim Hawkins, Long John and Ben Gunn all those years ago.

I can see Oscar Outlaw now. Above his desk he was all authority, his great lion head cradled in his hands, elbows on the desk and, between his elbows, the book. But below the desk he was all little boy. His bent knees bounced up and down. His legs were in frantic motion as a duck's legs are below the surface while the body remains calm above. Oscar Outlaw was treading water so as not to drown in the excitement of the stories.

Eventually, the day we all dreaded arrived. The start of the 11+ examinations! The whole affair was a blur at the time, but I remember the spelling part. One by one we had to go to the front of the class and stand beside Oscar Outlaw as he sat at his desk. On the desk were several sheets of paper with columns of words. As he pointed to a word we had to read it. The only word I remember is the word I had never seen or heard before. 'Antiku,' I said. It was 'antique'.

There couldn't have been many households in our village where antiques were part of tea-time conversation, but if there were, those were the children the Grammar School wanted.

There were a few posh kids in the area but they went away to school, and they went away for holidays. They hardly existed for us at all. We were the 'common boys' they shouldn't play with. We could spit further, pee higher.

The posh girls went to the riding stables, run by a strapping young lady called Tessa. We called her Tessy Titswobble. When her horse trotted her bosom galloped. I thought that if her horse jumped fences, Tessa would get black eyes.

A few children passed the exam and were told they would be going to the Grammar School. A few more were in a borderline group and had to go before an interview panel who would decide if they were Grammar School material or not. I was in this group.

I dreaded this day more than the days of exams. My mother gave my plimsolls a fresh coat of whitener and gave my hair another lick. I remember being ushered into the room and a row of old faces. That's all.

At school, a few days later, I noticed Oscar having a quiet word with two or three of the children who had also been for the interview. By the end of the day he had said nothing to me. I waited for the class to empty and approached his desk. 'Please, sir. Did I pass?'

Oscar looked at me over his spectacles. 'I'm afraid not,' he said.

I ran from the room, bounded down the stairs two at a time, which wasn't allowed, and burst out through the doors into the sunshine. I leapt and jumped and whooped down the road after my friends.

I hadn't passed! I was going to the Secondary Modern School with my mates. What a relief!

Then I remembered the bike. I would have to learn to ride the bike. If I had made it to the Grammar School I could have gone by bus.

Because the bus drivers, conductors and even inspectors drank tea in our shop, they let me travel free on the buses as often as I wanted. Sometimes on rainy days I just travelled up and down the entire route for hours watching the town going about its business.

Sometimes I took Sandy, and the two of us would get off the bus at the far north end of the town where a freshwater stream ran down a wooded valley to the beach. From there we could walk further north over dunes, on to beaches I thought of as a foreign country.

Boys are very territorial. The area where they live is *their* land, and strange children wandering into it should watch out. But here, at the smart north end of town, there seemed to be no children. Perhaps the children who lived here were rich kids who were sent away to school. If there were children around, they were too polite to bother a strange boy and a dog.

I had no real ambition at this time other than the dream of going to Hollywood or playing for England, except for one day when I went to a fun-fair in Great Yarmouth. There was a striptease lady in a tent. She posed naked in a golden frame, behind a filmy sheet which made it all fuzzy and artistic. If only I was a girl, I thought; that's what I would do when I grew up.

He took us sketching on the first day. Unbelievably he took us to the very church orchard I had been caught scrumping in a few years before. I knew the old Dracula vicar had left the village, and had been replaced by a roly-poly vicar who liked brown ale and sing-along in the Trowel and Hammer, so I wasn't alarmed.

Sketching those gnarled old apple trees was such fun I couldn't think why I had never done it before. Drawing had always been an indoor thing, flat out on the floor in front of the fire, making things up.

One day, I had a new customer on my newspaper round. He came to the door as I opened the gate. He said he had just arrived in the town from Yorkshire, and asked me if there was clay in the local cliffs. I said there was and we used to dig it out and make model tanks and planes from it. We stuck matchsticks in as guns and baked them hard in our mothers' ovens.

The new customer, Tom Hudson, asked me to bring a bucket of clay to the Art School, where he was a teacher. I knew nothing about the Art School except that it was above the local Youth Club, around the corner from my barber.

When I took the clay to Mr Hudson, he decided it was too gritty for modelling, or sculpture as he called it, but suggested I join a Saturday class he was starting for school children. It was free, so I did.

Because I couldn't ride a bike I delivered the newspapers to houses nearest the shop. Other paperboys went farther afield on their bikes.

If I had been able to ride a bike, I wouldn't have had the paper round nearest the shop. I wouldn't have met Tom Hudson. I would never have gone to art school.

My family gave up trying to get me to ride my bike, and my mother sold it. I had to walk to the Secondary School, about two miles away. There was a route to the school along a narrow lane, and while all the bike riders pedalled along the roads, I walked the muddy lane and enjoyed it; swordfighting imaginary highwaymen and chopping the heads of giant cow parsley.

The school was a long, single-storeyed red brick building. At one end was the Boys' School and at the other, the Girls' School. Down the middle of the playground was an imaginary line. Girls stayed on one side and boys on the other.

Playtime was the best part of school. Children came to the school from a wide area and there were several tough boys around. The group of boys from my old school stayed together, played together and fought together. There were lots of fights in the playground.

Fights usually started as a scuffle between two boys. A ring of boys would form around them and the cry, 'A fight! A fight!' made the ring of boys swell. Sometimes other boys became involved in the fight before teachers arrived to break it up.

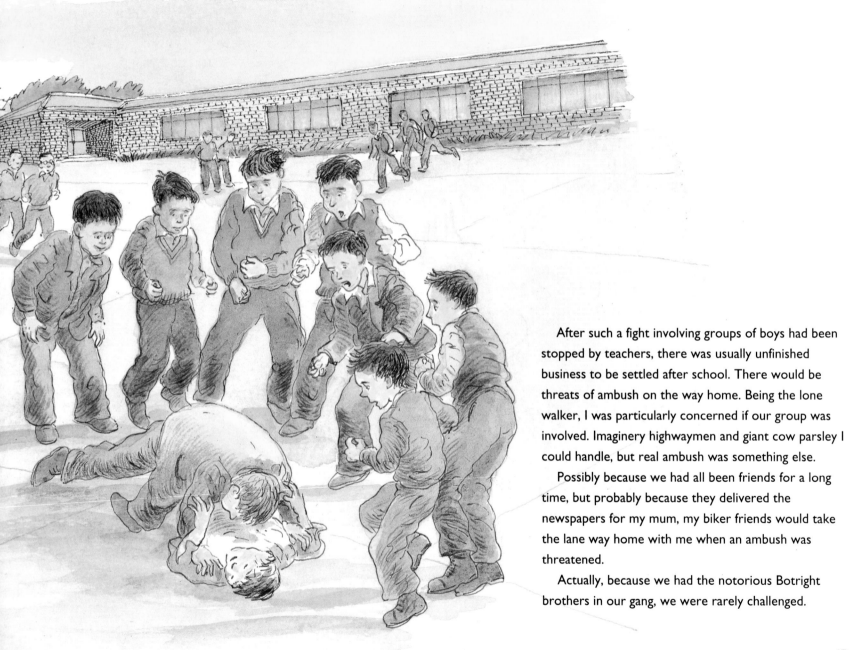

After such a fight involving groups of boys had been stopped by teachers, there was usually unfinished business to be settled after school. There would be threats of ambush on the way home. Being the lone walker, I was particularly concerned if our group was involved. Imaginery highwaymen and giant cow parsley I could handle, but real ambush was something else.

Possibly because we had all been friends for a long time, but probably because they delivered the newspapers for my mum, my biker friends would take the lane way home with me when an ambush was threatened.

Actually, because we had the notorious Botright brothers in our gang, we were rarely challenged.

The school was divided into four House teams, and teachers were assigned to each House. We boys didn't care which House ended the term with most House points, but to some of the teachers it seemed to be a matter of life or death. We got House points for playing in the school team, getting good marks, or for being helpful – filling the inkwells at the beginning of school, or closing the windows at the end of school.

Harry Woods, a big red-faced teacher with ginger hair and a ginger suit, was fanatical that his House should win the silver shield and only gave those jobs to boys in his House.

At about this time we got a new Headmaster. It was his first job as a Headmaster and he was full of new ideas.

He walked on to the stage on his first morning wearing his black academic gown. We were shocked. We had never seen anyone wear such a thing except in Will Hay comedy films. This man meant business. He was Michael Duane.

He wanted to brighten the place up. He asked the art teacher, Mr Nicholls, to select a couple of boys to design and paint a mural in the entrance to the school.

Mr Nicholls picked me and another boy, Brian Gifford. We did the mural of the local fishing industry: fishing boats, nets, etc. The Headmaster realized that I was good at not much beside art. He knew I was going to the Art School on Saturdays, and he arranged for me to go there two afternoons a week as well.

*Brian Gifford and I painting the mural.*

Most of the teachers at the Alderman Woodrow School expected little from us. The music teacher, whose name was Claude, expected more and was treated appallingly by us. He hated our accents and our manners. He was outraged if he saw us eating an apple in the street.

Claude made us push out our lips and form perfect O shapes with our mouths, then make an 'Ooh' sound, blowing gently at the same time. This, he hoped, would enable us to sing 'Nymphs and Shepherds' with a perfect BBC accent.

It all became too much for him and he left the school.

The new music teacher was very young and we treated him even worse than we had treated Claude. A few boys decided their voices were breaking so they were excused singing. Next week, we all said our voices were breaking. As we couldn't sing, the music teacher tried to tell us something of the history of music.

At some stage, and for a reason lost on me, he mentioned Michelangelo, and described him lying on his back painting the ceiling of the Sistine Chapel. From that day I was called Angelo, partly because of painting the school mural, but largely because my classmates thought I was having a lazy time at the Art School. And my name was Michael.

Some of the teachers were strict. One we respected was Arthur Rudd. We respected him because he was strict but fair. One day he discovered that none of us had read *The Wind in the Willows*. For the next few Friday afternoons he read from the book and we ruffians, big boys now with long trousers, were completely hooked by Ratty, Mole and all the inhabitants of the river bank.

When we got to the top of the school, our classroom was the one which joined the Girls' School end of the building. From our classroom we could see the girls playing netball. One girl in particular caught my attention. She was very good at netball and had a ponytail.

I found out her name was Molly. She was going out with a tall, good-looking boy in our class called Terry. He had dark, curly hair and wore a cricket sweater. He looked more like Grammar School material.

After the episode with Pud's canoe, I had no wish to have one of my own. Instead I got a lilo – an air-mattress. Although not as grown up as a canoe, it was actually more fun. Several of us could pile on at once, and you could dive from it.

One day, I was lying on my towel, stretched over the hot pebbles of the beach. In those summers the stones were sometimes too hot to walk on. People would hop and skip to the sea as if their feet were on fire. A shadow fell over me. I looked up. It was Brenda. I had sat next to Brenda for most of my years at Primary School. I had copied my sums from Brenda. Another reason I failed my exams.

She asked if she could borrow my lilo. She was wearing a shiny swimsuit with elasticated sides. When she brought the lilo back, the wet swimsuit showed the little dent of her bellybutton. Brenda had changed. I knew we would never play rugby together again.

Then I went to float on the lilo. It seemed different. It wasn't a galleon or a diving board any more. I put my head on the pillow and just lulled about on the dozing sea. Brenda had lain on my mattress . . . Then I felt a stinging pain on my face. I hadn't noticed a jellyfish tentacle clinging to the pillow.

Just when you are feeling good about a girl you get stung.

In addition to making drawings of football matches and battles, I sometimes painted posters for the shop, advertising various products, like a new washing powder or fruit drink.

One of the posh customers, Mrs Garood, thought her nephew in London should know about this. He was an executive in a big advertising agency in London and Mrs Garood arranged for Mum and me to have an interview at his office.

The school agreed for me to have a day off and we travelled up on the train. I wonder what the poor man thought of his aunt forcing him to see this little kid with his scruffy pictures.

He was very nice. We sat in his splendid office and he said I should keep drawing, study hard, and perhaps in a few years he would see me again.

*I was always attracted by the graphics on the labels in the shop. Spratts dog food was my favourite.*

Mum and I spent the rest of the day at the Festival of Britain. It was staged on the South Bank of the Thames (the Festival Hall is the only part of the great jamboree that remains) and was officially described as 'A Tonic for the Nation'.

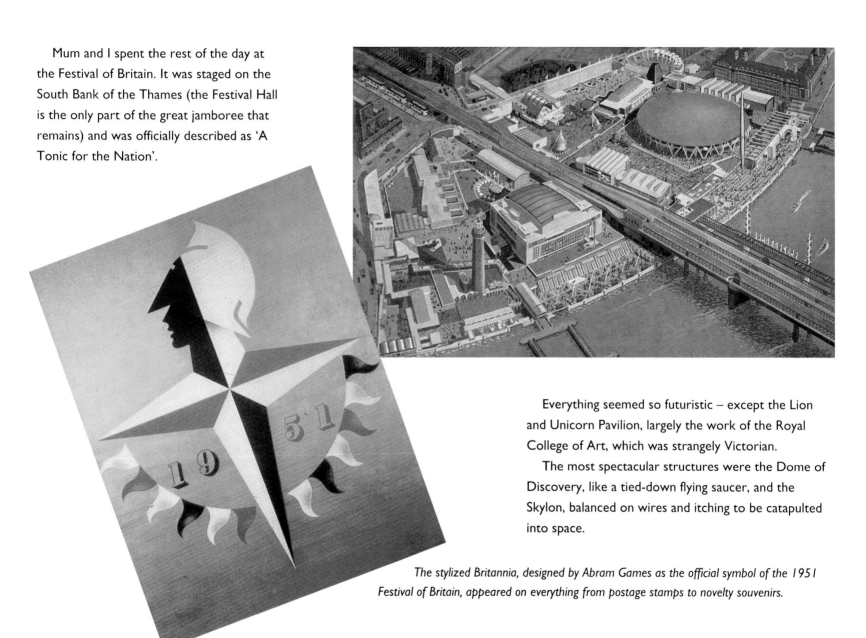

Everything seemed so futuristic – except the Lion and Unicorn Pavilion, largely the work of the Royal College of Art, which was strangely Victorian.

The most spectacular structures were the Dome of Discovery, like a tied-down flying saucer, and the Skylon, balanced on wires and itching to be catapulted into space.

*The stylized Britannia, designed by Abram Games as the official symbol of the 1951 Festival of Britain, appeared on everything from postage stamps to novelty souvenirs.*

My lasting memories are of the special rock with the Festival symbol through the middle (Mum said it was expensive at one shilling and sixpence) and that the whole event was overcrowded and over pink. The view across the river of sooty St Paul's standing solitary among vast black bomb sites was more intriguing. I knew the bomb sites would be full of marigolds and 'common boys' inventing worlds more imaginative and lasting than the pink fly-away shapes at the Festival.

In class next day Mr Rudd asked if I had been offered
the Managing Director's job at the advertising agency,
ha, ha. I realized then that the teachers thought it was
ridiculous that a boy like me should have such
ambitions.

In those days very few people had cars. Only posh people. If ordinary folk wanted to go on an outing they had to go by train or coach. The old coaches were called charabancs. I don't know why, but they were fun. Occasionally on a Sunday afternoon in summer, Mum, Aunt Louie and I would go on an outing. (My brothers, Pud and Ivan, were old enough to have adventures of their own.)

We went wherever the charabanc was going. Sometimes it was a 'Mystery Tour', when only the driver knew the destination, but as the destination was always a pub, no one was worried. The outing was the thing and we would sing all the way home.

My favourite charabanc destination was a remote barn of a pub called The Eel's Foot. It was beside a wide river, or broad, and we could hire rowing boats and trail arms and legs in the rippling colours of the setting sun.

Eventually Mum bought a car – a tiny Austin. Mum couldn't drive and had no intention of learning. Ivan and Pud could drive because they worked at the garage, and the plan was that they would take turns to drive Mum on outings every Sunday afternoon. The rest of us piled in the back.

Now we could go where the charabancs didn't. Best of all we could visit Granny Bacon. She was Mum's mother and was the landlady of a pub in deepest Norfolk. She was the classic country granny. Small, very tough, dressed always in black and wearing a silver brooch at her neck with the words 'Mother' on it. Her grey hair was gathered back into a bun with huge steel pins, and she wore a tall, black pointy hat.

Her mother had been landlady at the pub, and when she became too old, Granny took over. She served the customers, washed the glasses, scrubbed the brick floors and looked after the cellar, and the large family.

Grandfather had a bad leg and Granny used to smother it in a daily poultice of boiled watercress which the children had to scour the countryside to find.

Everything inside the pub seemed brown. The locals had gnarled brown hands, tobacco-stained, droopy moustaches and yellow teeth like horses. They spat plugs of chewing tobacco into the spittoons under the brown wooden settles, and their boots trailed mud over the brick floors. Even the plants on the windowsills were nicotine stained and gasped in the thick smoke, gazing longingly at the fresh air outside. When the sun came through the window it turned into a golden haze through which flitted the tiny black shadow of Granny Bacon, darting from cellar to bar with big pots of brown beer. Granny's pub, The Fox and Hounds, was one of the smells of childhood.

At the back of the pub, Granny Bacon maintained a huge garden. Every kind of fruit, vegetable and herb grew in wild profusion. There were golden gooseberries as big as ping-pong balls. Bees buzzed between bushes dangling blackcurrants and redcurrants. Below them trailed the big leaves and trumpet flowers of marrows and squashes. Pear trees towered above old apple trees bent under loads of apples with weird and wonderful names.

There was a three-holer toilet in the garden of the pub for the customers, and a one-holer for Granny and the family.

Big red hens hid eggs everywhere, and in the public bar, in a glass case, was an ostrich egg as big as a rugby ball. Beneath the case, old men played dominoes and I could imagine Granny Bacon giving them the odd spell along with their beer — magic potions to make their hens lay eggs as large as ostrich eggs.

In 1953 there was a terrible storm, and a huge tide raged down the North Sea, destroying sea defences and flooding the low land. Many people drowned along the east coast and in Holland, where the dykes burst.

The cliffs of Pakefield were high enough to prevent flooding but much of the cliff was washed away. The sea surged over the Lowestoft sea wall and through the old beach village part of the town.

No one drowned there although some of the little cottages were left full of sand and mud to a depth of several feet. Big boys were given a few days off school to help dig out the old cottages. We pretended to be an international rescue team. We were too late to save a hutch full of rabbits and lots of dolls and teddy bears.

Damaged by High Seas at Pakefield.

High Tide Damage at Pakefield, Suffolk.

As soon as I was fifteen I could leave school. With the encouragement of my
Headmaster and Tom Hudson, Mum agreed that I could go full-time to the
Art School. I was very lucky. I was the youngest son. Pud and Ivan were both
working and earning enough to keep themselves and give some to Mum.
Between them, they could afford for me to go to Art School.

On my first day I went into a drawing studio with the other students, who
were two or three years older than me. A lady came in and took off all her
clothes. She stood on a little box in the middle of the room.
The students stood behind easels and began to draw. I stood behind an
easel in the far corner and sharpened my pencil. It kept breaking.

Because it was a very small Art School I couldn't study all the subjects I needed. So one day each week I travelled to the Art School at Great Yarmouth and sometimes to the Art School at Ipswich.

In East Anglia in the 1950s there were not many ladies around who would take off their clothes to model. In fact, Sadie was the only one. So Sadie was also in demand at the neighbouring art schools, and the two of us spent long hours cuddled up together in country buses winding along the cold, foggy roads of Norfolk and Suffolk.

Painting the same person over and over for month after month teaches you about seeing and reading colour. I had no idea there were so many pinks, blues, yellows, ochres and mauves in flesh. A couple of years later we had a new model, Lily. She was paler, cooler-coloured than Sadie and needed quite a different mix of colours. Her bone structure was more apparent. We drew all or parts of the skeleton repeatedly. The ball and socket of the thigh bone and pelvis, wrists and knuckles, elbows and ankles. It was very boring but we didn't question it.

When we came to draw and paint Lily, we saw the value of all the skeleton drawings.

November 1954

85

I think myself lucky to have gone to a small Art School still steeped in tradition. We studied anatomy, perspective, colour theory, the history of art and architecture. We were also out in all weathers drawing the world around us.

The Lowestoft fish market was a favourite subject. It was so noisy and frantic and friendly.

Time and again we painted the same orchard, in all seasons. The winter was best. There are so many colours in snow; so many blues, browns, reds in the black trees.

Gradually Tom Hudson led us into total abstraction. Starting with the trees in the orchard, step by step, until painting and constructing abstracts seemed natural and made perfect sense.

He urged us to draw the 'particular', the basic, the essence of a form or movement. We studied the structure of plants as we had the skeleton, opened seed pods and drew the tiny seeds very large. Isolated on paper or canvas, the seed seemed as big as the world.

At the end of my first term at the Art School a big Christmas party was organized. It was Fancy Dress and everyone had to perform a party piece. Some of the new students didn't want to do a solo performance so we decided to form a band. We had no instruments so we made our own. As I had access to biscuit tins I made drums, so I was the drummer.

When Tom Hudson added our act to the bill he wrote down 'Jazz Band'. I felt a shock of excitement. That's it. 'Jazz Band'. Of course, we were awful, but we were hooked. After the party, we all bought real instruments, except we used a tea chest and broom handle instead of double-bass. We felt this was more traditional anyway. Jazz took over from football. We were jazz fans now.

At the start of my second year, a few new students arrived. I recognized one of them. She was Molly, the girl with the ponytail.

There were two distinct groups at the local Jazz Club. One group was there for the jazz. The other group was there for the beer. There was a late licence on jazz nights so drunks could come from all the pubs around and drink later in the Jazz Club. Most of this group were young fishermen or 'fisherboys'.

The 'teddy boys' in the mid 1950s adopted a unique clothes style. They wore long drape jackets with lapels and cuffs in contrasting colours, narrow 'drain pipe' trousers and big suede shoes with thick crêpe soles. On the front of the shoe there was often a glittery chain. Their shirts were plain coloured, pink or pale yellow with a narrow 'slim jim' tie or a 'bootlace' tie.

In our area, the fisherboys had their own distinctive fashion too. Their jackets were similar in shape to the teds', but even more special, with double pleats in the back and a half belt. The trousers were the opposite of drain pipes, and had very wide legs. They were very expensive. The fisherboys, like generations of seamen before them, wore a single earring (forty years before earrings became trendy). Earrings were worn by seafarers to pay for a proper Christian burial should their bodies be washed up on a foreign shore.

The fisherboys were often at sea for many days and nights in harsh and dangerous conditions. When they came ashore for a day or two, they had a pocket full of money and a short time in which to spend it. They lavished their hard-earned cash on suits, girlfriends and a good time.

Many of my schoolmates became fisherboys. I envied them their money, but not their life on the rough, freezing North Sea.

91

There were frequent fights between the 'fisherboys' and the 'teddy boys', but the musicians were usually regarded as neutrals. But one night while our band was playing the fight erupted onto the stage.

Mike, our clarinet player, always stared into space while he played. During one long solo he was staring vacantly as usual when one of the fisherboys took exception. He thought Mike was staring at his glass eye. The fisherboy leapt on to the stage and butted Mike in the face. He was followed by several of his brothers, all notoriously violent, and the rest of the fisherboys.

Drums and bodies rolled around the floor as the teddy boys waded in, and the musicians, all notoriously timid, escaped. Except Colin, our vegetarian pacifist banjo player who stayed behind to point out that fighting was silly.

Our band never got better than awful, but we got 'gigs' as the interval band at various pubs and clubs. Of course, the interval was when everyone went to the bar to get more drink, so very few people ever heard how bad we were.

The best 'gigs' were the 'Riverboat Shuffles', named after the traditional riverboats which carried bands and revellers up and down the Mississippi. Our boats were the last of the lovely old steamers which chugged along the River Waveney and into the network of broads. There would be two or three bands on board, crates of beer and mad dancing. The boat stopped at remote waterside pubs where we played and drank and sailed home in the dark.

The Jazz Club became a weekly haunt for us. Most of the art students went there, including Molly. I tried to think of ways to impress her. Maybe, I thought, next time we go sketching on the pier she might fall in and I could rescue her and have an excuse to talk to her.

But one night, Molly and I didn't go to the pub. Everyone else had gone but I found myself standing on a corner with Molly and her drop handlebar racing bike. We seemed to talk for ages. It was misty and cold. I don't know what we talked about. Then she kissed me, hopped on her bike and disappeared into the mist.

I ran down the road, leaping in the air and punching the overhanging autumn leaves. I ran all the way home without touching the ground. The last time I had been kissed was by my brother Ivan's friend Bob's wife at her wedding when I was nine years old.

Then gloom, fear. If I was to 'go out' with Molly, I would have to learn to ride a bike . . .

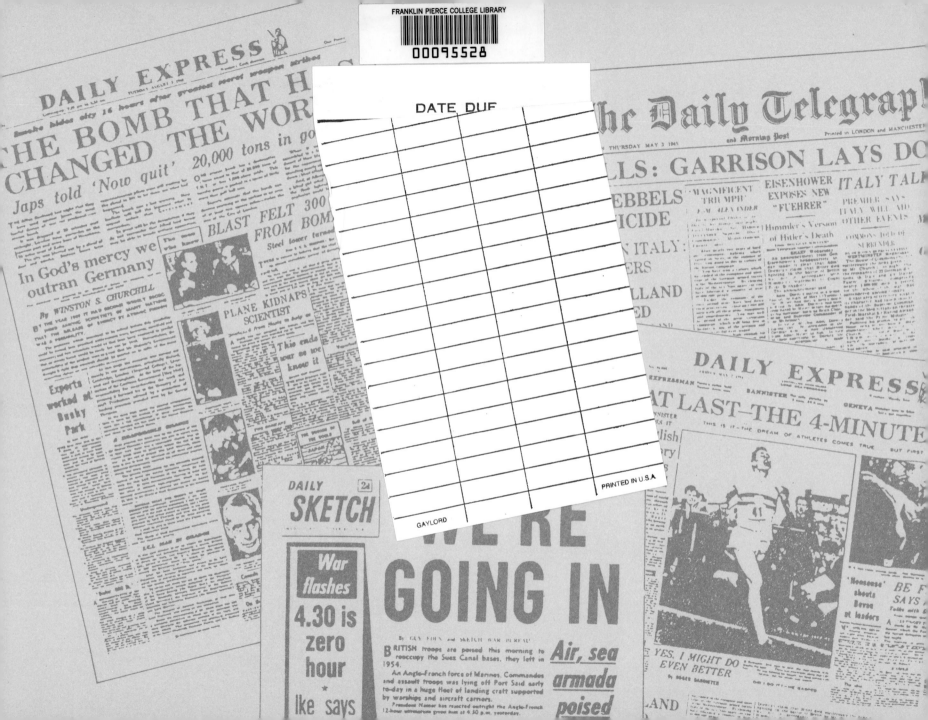

FRANKLIN PIERCE COLLEGE LIBRARY

00095528

DATE DUE

GAYLORD

PRINTED IN U.S.A.